# CALMING THE MIND

*Tibetan Buddhist Teachings on*
*Cultivating Meditative Quiescence*

# CALMING THE MIND

*Tibetan Buddhist Teachings on*
*Cultivating Meditative Quiescence*

by Gen Lamrimpa (Ven. Jampal Tenzin)

Translated by B. Alan Wallace
Edited by Hart Sprager

Snow Lion Publications
Ithaca, New York USA

Snow Lion Publications
P.O. Box 6483
Ithaca, New York 14851
USA

First Published as *Śamatha Meditation*.

Printed in USA.

ISBN 1-55939-051-4

**Library of Congress Cataloging-in-Publication Data**
Gen Lamrimpa. 1934-
   Samatha meditation : Tibetan Buddhist teachings on cultivat-
ing meditative quiescence
(Ven. Jampel Tenzin) ; translated by B. Alan Wallace ; edited by
Hart Sprager.
    p. cm.
   Translated from Tibetan.
   Includes index.
   ISBN 1-55939-051-4
   1. Meditation—Buddhism.  2. Śamatha (Buddhism)  3. Bud-
dhism—China—Tibet—Doctrines.  I. Sprager, Hart.
  BQ7805.G46   1992
294.3'443—dc20                    92-28543
                                   CIP

# Contents

# Editor's Note

On January 6, 1988, at Cloud Mountain Retreat Center in Castle Rock, Washington, a group of twenty-four American dharma students and aspiring meditators began a śamatha retreat under the guiding hand of the Tibetan lama Gen Lamrimpa (the Venerable Jampal Tenzin). Some of us had made a three-month commitment to the practice, others of us were there for six months, and eight of us had committed ourselves to a year of meditation.

The body of this work is made up of the teachings on śamatha Gen Lamrimpa gave during the first two weeks of the retreat. Those teachings were based on *The Great Exposition of the Stages of the Path of Awakening* by Tsong-kha-pa, who in turn based his teachings largely on Maitreya's text *Examination of the Center and the Extremes*.

Gen Lamrimpa included teachings by Asaṅga, namely his text called *The Stages of the Listeners* and the teachings of Śāntarakṣita on *The Essence of the Center*. In addition he included teachings by Kamalaśīla—*The States of Meditation*, as well as the *Compendium of Practices*.

All of these teachers, as well as Śantideva (whom Gen Lamrimpa quotes many times during the teachings), had perfectly attained śamatha during their lifetimes. At the time the teachings were given, Gen Lamrimpa himself had twenty years' experience in śamatha and other meditative practices.

Transferring a teacher's words to paper is a relatively simple process but anyone who has experienced them must realize that the task of transferring to the printed page the vibrance and vitality present in the oral transmissions of a true master is next to impossible. Recognizing the impossibilities inherent in the task, all of us who have worked on this book have been motivated by the wish to pass on the essence of the teachings as well as the fundamentally unique quality of Gen Lamrimpa's presentation.

Throughout the teachings, Gen Lamrimpa began the day by speaking about motivation and the ways in which we, his students, could use the proper motivation to enhance our own internal processing of what we were about to hear. While what he said invariably enhanced our motivation, it sometimes seemed to have less than a direct relationship to the subject of śamatha. In that motivation is such an essential aspect of the practice, there was simply no way or reason to exclude those motivational moments from this edition. Four chapters—six, eight, ten and twelve—have been compiled from these daily teachings.

In his teachings, Gen Lamrimpa demonstrated his ability to present technical and often complicated material in a very uncomplicated and down-to-earth manner, and one of Alan Wallace's most outstanding qualities as a translator is his ability to transform that down-to-earth presentation into truly vernacular English while at the same time retaining the precision of the terminology and exactitude of the concepts being presented. It is my hope that the delicate balance they were able to create is evident in this rendering.

Finally, Gen Lamrimpa constantly emphasized the importance of continuity. At the same time, he took the liberty to digress from the formal outline of the presentation whenever such a digression enhanced the understanding of his students. Those digressions, which turned out to be shortcuts to the very heart of the matter, are included here just as they came up in the teachings.

It may be helpful for the reader to know a little about the basic daily routine we followed during the retreat. It was very much of an accordion-style schedule, devised so that each of us could function as much as possible on our own time clock. We awoke at five a.m. and went to sleep at around ten p.m. Except for hour-and-a-half breaks for breakfast, lunch and dinner, and short tea breaks throughout the day, we were urged to devote every waking minute to the practice. We were encouraged to maintain silence in all group areas, such as the dining hall, and to avoid contact with one another. We meditated individually in our own rooms. We started meditating in fifteen-minute sessions and took a fifteen-minute break between sessions, plus an occasional longer tea break as it seemed necessary. This format allowed for as many as eighteen quarter-hour sessions throughout the day at the beginning of the retreat, a total of four and a half hours of actual meditation in what would ideally be a full day of practice.

As our proficiency in the practice increased, we extended the length of the sessions but held firm on the length of the break. At the end of a year of practice, some meditators were doing sessions that extended well beyond two hours. Thus, the time of formal meditation increased from the base four and a half hours to somewhere between six and twelve hours per day, depending on the individual's progress.

For the length of our stay at Cloud Mountain, whatever that length was, we were guided and nurtured by Gen Lamrimpa, by his translator and assistant teacher Alan Wallace, and his attendant and translator, Thubten Jampa. All of our physical needs were attended to by the marvelous Cloud Mountain staff—David and Anna Branscomb, Brittany Faulkner, Janet Thomas and Tom Diggs—and the many volunteers from the Seattle area. In truth, the entire experience was made possible through their efforts as well as the efforts of the Dharma Friendship Foundation, which sponsored the retreat, and its president, Chris Borland. And special thanks to Pauly Fitze and Vana Jakic, who transcribed the tapes of Gen Lamrimpa's teachings. To all of them we owe the greatest debt of gratitude for the opportunity they provided us to study and meditate, and to make this written record of the teachings a reality.

**PART I**
**INTRODUCTION TO**
**THE TEACHINGS**

# 1  Prelude to the Practice

The practice of *śamatha*,* sometimes translated as *meditative quiescence* or *calm abiding*, is not unique to Buddhism. It is common to non-Buddhist traditions as well. In fact, it is an essential aspect of most spiritual meditative practices because meditative quiescence is an indispensable tool essential for attaining liberation, *nirvāṇa*,* or the full awakening of buddhahood.

These are lofty goals, and many obstacles lie in the path of anyone who seeks them. The chief obstacles to liberation are known as afflictive obstructions. The chief obstacles to the full awakening of a buddha are known as cognitive obstructions. They are the collective obstacles to omniscience, and to go beyond them one must apply the proper antidote. In the case of both the afflictive and cognitive obstacles, that antidote is the realization of emptiness.

In and of itself, the realization of emptiness is a lofty goal, and the attainment of the wisdom that realizes emptiness requires an extremely stable mind able to focus on the ultimate truth.

*Pronounced "sha-ma-ta." The Tibetan terms and explanations for words marked with an asterisk can be found in the glossary.

What does that term, "extremely stable mind," mean?

It means a mind sufficiently stable to be able to focus upon emptiness without wavering to any other object. In order to cultivate such a stable mind capable of focusing upon emptiness without wavering to any other phenomenon, śamatha, or meditative quiescence, is indispensable.

Equally indispensable for the attainment of the state of śamatha is proper motivation. This is the first step in the process, the cultivation of a proper motivation that will create a momentum to carry the meditator through the course of the practice, however long it may last.

The primary objective of cultivating śamatha is the attainment of liberation and full awakening as a means to be of service to others. However, there are subsidiary effects or benefits of meditative quiescence, namely the development of psychic powers and other forms of heightened awareness. These *siddhis*,* too, can be used in the service of others. However, it is important to remember that the primary reason for the cultivation of śamatha is the attainment of liberation or full awakening.

In order to focus in on the proper motivation, one must ask the question: What is the point of attaining the full awakening of a buddha?

Just as space is without limit, so it is true that sentient beings are without limit. Buddhist cosmology says that among the various realms inhabited by sentient beings the majority abide in the hell realms, a smaller number abide in the realm of tormented spirits or *pretas*,* still fewer in the animal realms, still fewer in the human realm, fewer yet in the realm of the demi-gods and a very few in the *deva*\* world. Moreover, there are limitless numbers of beings in the intermediate state between death and rebirth who are not classified in any of the six realms of existence.

If we look at this question from a Western perspective, using all the available scientific technology, we see that although the ground is solid it is permeated by various types of organisms, as is the air, as is the water. Taking the Western scientific perspective one step further, it is said that something like a billion organisms live in the human body. So again we have the sense of a limitless number of sentient beings stretching infinitely into space.

Now, let us return to the Buddhist perspective and ask this question: What is the point of attaining the full awakening of a buddha? The answer is almost too obvious. Upon attaining full awakening, it is possible to be of unimaginable benefit to countless sentient beings, especially to those who have a close relationship with one's own being, the organisms in one's own body. Undoubtedly there is a close relationship with those.

If you were able to release from *saṃsāra*\* simply the billion organisms in your own body, that would be a tremendous achievement. To attain full awakening each would need to develop *bodhicitta,*\* the awakening mind, and in order to do that it is virtually necessary to have a human body. Imagine bringing each of these sentient beings with whom you have this intimate connection to the brink of full awakening by affording them the opportunity just to be born with a human body. Each would also have a billion organisms within it. A billion times a billion beings offered the opportunity of liberation by the act and motivation of a single individual.

In the abstract, the motivation of bodhicitta, the aspiration to attain full enlightenment for the benefit of all sentient beings, may seem impractical and impossible. However, looking at it from the perspective of our interdependence with just the beings within our own bodies can put the impossible within reach.

The quest for the attainment of *nirvāṇa* or liberation is chiefly discussed in the Hīnayāna\* scriptures. When one investigates this issue of liberation, it is helpful to look back to the preceding life as well as the lives preceding that life. That investigation will lead to an understanding that there is no beginning to one's previous lives, that life is indeed limitless.

If you follow the rim of a metal disc you will see that it has no end and no beginning. Saṃsāra, or the cycle of existence, is very much like the rim of that metal disc. Its beginning and its end cannot be found. It is our mental distortions and the actions conditioned by them that propel us through the endless cycles of saṃsāra. It is a self-perpetuating process.

While this is true of the cycle of life, it is possible to search for and find the beginning of one specific lifetime.

What is the origin of the specific human rebirth?

It is ignorance.

If we take this present body as an example, whence does it arise? It arises from ignorance, from ignorance and *karma*,* from the distorted action of a person of the same continuum as ourselves in a previous life. There was the ignorance; there was the action; it gave rise to this birth.

And whence arose that ignorance, that karma? It arose from preceding ignorance, from preceding karma, preceding without beginning.

Speaking of the twelve links of dependent origination, the great sage Asaṅga points out that the three primary mental afflictions—attachment, aversion and ignorance—arise from two types of karma—accomplishing and propulsive karma. These both arise from ignorance. The three interact in a self-perpetuating, beginningless, endless cycle. In this manner then, saṃsāra is a cycle without beginning and without end.

If one reflects upon the unsatisfactory nature of suffering, one finds that it too is beyond all bounds. Suffering is not something we like to look into very much. When we do look, however, we see how pervasive it is. Even if one has a quite pleasant human rebirth, even then the extent of suffering is immense. First there is the suffering of the very process of birth. Then following birth there are times of frustration when a child's desires go unfulfilled, the suffering of the discipline that forces the child to conform to its parents' and society's norms. The suffering continues through youth, as one goes to school and struggles to get good grades, all the sufferings of growing up, the suffering of not attracting the boy you like, or the suffering of getting the girl you like and finding she is not the person you wanted, but only the person you thought you wanted.

The suffering continues in adulthood. It becomes the suffering of seeking work, of seeking work that seems meaningful, of economic survival, trying to get one's act together, trying to get one's possessions together, struggling for success and attaining it. Eventually, when you have everything together, even when you're all set with success and everything you told yourself you wanted, then you have to protect it from all those who would take it from you if they had half the chance. Then you die, and you are back to being a beggar again, a baby again, coming into the world naked and without even a single possession.

This is the case in the human situation with a very pleasant human rebirth. But look at the beings with less fortunate human rebirths, at beings in the hell realms, in the preta realm, in the animal realm. There is yet more suffering in those.

At this point, each of us has had limitless experience in both lower and fortunate realms. But where has it gotten us? Right here, even in this fortunate situation in which we have the leisure to devote time and energy to spiritual practice, we are still subject to suffering. How much good has all that suffering done us?

We do not and can not stop it by saying, "I've gone through limitless lives. I've had my share. I'm satisfied with that. I think I'll move on now, on to something else." The truth is that we helplessly cultivate the very sources of our sorrow, we continue to be subject to suffering regardless of how much suffering we have had in the past, and continuing in this way we are bound to experience more suffering than we want to experience in the future.

On the one hand there is the suffering we have discussed. On the other, there are also sources of pleasure and happiness. Paradoxically, however, in the midst of the struggle to maintain happiness, to insure the continuance of pleasure, or pervaded by dissatisfaction with pleasures that have become familiar, these too become part of suffering.

When does this continuum of suffering end? It ends with the cessation of ignorance which brings about the attainment of liberation or nirvāṇa. If we truly seek happiness for ourselves it is that liberation that we should aim for. In the freedom from suffering that comes with liberation lies the true sense of happiness.

Considering all this, as we embark on a one-year retreat, a three-month retreat, or any other form of śamatha practice, what objective, what aspiration shall we hold in our mind? What motivation shall we choose?

## UNSUITABLE MOTIVATIONS

If our motivation is the increase of our reputation, greater acquisitions, praise, affluence, etc., then our whole practice will be less than insignificant. Moreover such a motivation will make the attainment of śamatha impossible.

What is the attainment of śamatha?

It is the access concentration* to the first *dhyāna*,* the first meditative stabilization. This belongs to a different dimension of existence known as the form realm. The prerequisite to the attainment of that dhyāna is the turning away from sensual desires. If the motivation for attainment entails attachment to the sensual or desire realm, then that very motivation for the practice becomes the primary obstacle to attainment.

Another unsuitable motivation is the personal satisfaction that comes from serving others. A doctor, for instance, serves others; but if his principal motivation for serving is the satisfaction he himself receives by serving and healing others, his effort becomes self-serving and self-centered. That motivation is centered entirely on benefits attainable only within this lifetime.

This kind of motivation would be equally unsuitable for the cultivation of śamatha. If one works to attain śamatha in order to bring benefit to other beings but is ultimately interested in the personal satisfaction to be gained through that seemingly altruistic act, that too is said to be an aspiration entailing concerns of this life, and it will become an obstacle for the cultivation of meditative quiescence.

You might logically ask if we are supposed to forget this lifetime all together. If I attain śamatha, will it bring no benefit in this lifetime?

This is not the case. If we turn our awareness to having a higher, truly altruistic aspiration, the benefits in this lifetime inevitably occur without any special thought or effort on our part. The lives of the historical Buddha, Buddha Śākyamuni, and the great pandits and contemplatives of India, Tibet, Thailand, Burma and China are the proof of the pudding. Some sought to attain the full awakening of a buddha, others strove for liberation, others hoped for favorable future lives. All these motivations extended beyond this life, yet their effectiveness in serving others in this lifetime was immense.

One of the most well-known examples might be the Tibetan yogi and saint, Milarepa. A teacher of great renown and reputation, he is esteemed by Tibetan Buddhists of every order. Milarepa had utterly renounced the concerns of this life. His objective was very simply to attain full awakening for the benefit of all creatures. His renunciation was complete. He dispensed with all concerns for food, clothing, reputation, all mundane affairs. Paradoxically, he became the recipient of all the things he had renounced.

When most people get ill they want to make sure everyone knows about it, for the sake of sympathy, or in the hope that they will get the best care, the best hospitals, the best doctors. When they're on their death bed, they want comfort, want their loved ones around them. Many think a big funeral will be the best funeral. Still others leave intricate instructions on what should be done with their remains, insuring that a lot of people will be concerned with their bodies after death.

Milarepa's attitude was completely opposite. In one of his songs, he said, "When I am ill, may no one know about it; when I die, may there be no one to weep; and when I am dead, may there be no one who has to dispose of my body." At the end of his life, word of his final illness spread far and wide.

In spite of his wishes his disciples came from every corner of the country to be with him at the moment of death and weep for him. After he died there was great concern over his remains. The *ḍākas* and *ḍākinīs** wanted them; his students and disciples wanted them; the people from the village in which he had been born wanted them.

On the surface one might think that if one simply concerns oneself with altruistic intent and future lifetimes, the practical aspects of this life will not be accomplished, and one will be a failure. This simply isn't true. On the contrary, when one really does renounce or let go of this lifetime everything is taken care of by force of the deeper motivation.

## MEANINGFUL MOTIVATIONS

There are three levels of meaningful or authentic motivation for the practice of śamatha:

—To attain rebirth in the form or formless realms
—To attain liberation or nirvāṇa
—To attain full awakening

## REBIRTH IN THE FORM OR FORMLESS REALMS

Such a rebirth can result in a life that lasts billions of earthly years and is filled with tremendous bliss. The first four dhyānas in the formless realm, as well as the fourth to the eighth, are so subtle that it is almost like being in a deep, blissful sleep.

Some non-Buddhist contemplatives confuse rebirth in either of these two realms with the attainment of nirvāṇa. With that in mind, they make its attainment the motivation for their practice of śamatha. To strive for that is still of greater meaning than simply striving to attain śamatha as a means of accomplishing the affairs of this life. However, if you follow this route and obtain such an exalted rebirth, after so many billions of years when the power of the śamatha that got you there is exhausted, you fall from that blissful state and quite possibly could be reborn in the hell realms. Looking at its culmination, such a rebirth seems less significant. It simply decays until one falls back again.

## LIBERATION OR NIRVĀṆA

Liberation, or nirvāṇa, irrevocably cuts the continuum and source of one's own suffering. It is a very powerful motivation and a magnificent attainment. Upon attaining nirvāṇa, while abiding in meditative equipoise, one is of no evident benefit to any other sentient being. One is in a state of total inactivity.

There are many accounts of beings who have attained liberation being stimulated to seek and attain the full awakening of a buddha. But it is said that it is far more difficult for such a person to attain full awakening than it is for a person who has not attained liberation.

Why is that?

Liberated beings are so free of suffering, so totally beyond suffering, that it is difficult for them to develop any sense of empathy or sympathy for those who do suffer. Thus, it is difficult for them to generate great compassion or bodhicitta, also essential prerequisites for the attainment of full awakening.

## FULL AWAKENING

Of the three authentic motivations for engaging in the practice of śamatha, the altruistic aspiration for full awakening is the most meaningful. In terms of altruism or serving the welfare of others, even if one is not engaged in an actual activity, in some active service, it lifts the practice to the highest level. Āryadeva says that the aspiration to serve, in and of itself, is an aspect or means of serving others.

We see that there are basically two avenues to the attainment of full awakening. One is to attain liberation, remain there for some time, get stimulated, get back into gear, and then go on to seek full awakening. The other is simply and directly to go to full awakening. This being the case, why not take the direct path?

It is very much an individual choice. Some may simply feel overwhelmed because the enlightenment of a buddha may seem to be beyond reach. To such a person it might seem more practical to say, "I could handle liberation," and go in that direction. If one has the feeling that it would be more appropriate or satisfactory simply to attain liberation, then let that be the motivation. Remember, however, that through that attainment you really check out of society; that is, you are free of birth, out of the world—at least for a time.

Apart from that special kind of attitude one might as well strive for full awakening for the benefit of all creatures from the outset and then think of śamatha as the instrument for attaining that goal.

The actual attainment of bodhicitta, or the awakening mind, is difficult. However, insofar as we can cultivate the motivation to attain full awakening for the benefit of others, that very motivation and the practices ensuing from it are a means of service to others. It will be worthwhile for us to cultivate that motivation, for this year, this month, this day, for this hour in order to bring this attitude of motivation to the conscious part of the mind. We should try to cultivate such an attitude at the beginning of each meditation session.

To generate the motivation to attain full enlightenment for the benefit of others, first take refuge by reciting the verses of refuge three times:

> I go for refuge, until I am enlightened, to the Buddha,
>     the Dharma, the Sangha.
> Through the virtuous merit that I collect by practicing
>     giving and other perfections,
> May I attain the state of the Buddha in order to benefit
>     all sentient beings.

Next, recite the verses of the Four Immeasurables:

May all beings know happiness and the causes of
  happiness.
May all beings be free from suffering and the causes
  of suffering.
May all beings never be separated from the great
  happiness that is beyond all misery.
May all beings dwell in equanimity, unaffected by
  attraction and aversion.

Cultivate this motivation in the midst of the session as well.
When the mind is wandering off, let that cultivation bring it
back to the meditation. At the conclusion of each session it
is important to dedicate the merit of that specific session,
saying:

Let this merit represent all of my merit, past, present and future, and may all of this merit be dedicated
towards the full attainment of awakening for the benefit of all beings.

Finally, it is said to be most beneficial to end each session
with a prayer of dedication:

Just as the Buddhas and the Bodhisattvas of the three
times have dedicated their merit, so may my merit
go for the same events and projects to which they have
dedicated theirs.

For those of you who practice the Six-Session Guru Yoga,*
it will be to your advantage to begin some of your śamatha
sessions with one of the guru yoga sessions. At the point where
your guru* dissolves into your body and you then generate
yourself as Vajradhara (in the form of the blue Vajrasattva with
consort), it would be best to continue your śamatha practice
as Vajradhara. Then, at the end of the practice, do the dedication of merit.

# 2 Guidelines for Practice

The attainment of śamatha requires many favorable causes and conditions. Effort, no matter how great that effort might be, isn't enough. Many other things have to come together.

In the tantric* context, the practice of Vajrayāna,* realization arises in the stream of one's being through the blessing of one's spiritual mentor. Even that empowerment, by itself, is not sufficient. First one must eliminate the unfavorable circumstances of negative imprints from unwholesome acts. Second, one must acquire the positive influence of favorable imprints born of wholesome acts, i.e., merit. Third, one needs to engage in the practice by focusing on the objects of meditation.

Focusing the mind on the object of meditation is like planting the seed for the arisal of the realization. Eliminating unfavorable circumstances of unwholesome mental imprints is like making sure the seed is healthy and able to perform the essential function of a seed, giving rise to the sprout. The accumulation of merit might be likened to caring for the seed—giving it moisture, fertilizer and warmth.

When it meets with favorable circumstances, the healthy seed will give rise to a sprout. In the same way, when one focuses on the practice and encounters favorable circumstances—the accumulation of merit and the elimination of unwholesome imprints—the sprout of realization may arise.

## THE SEVEN-LIMB PŪJA

The Seven-Limb Pūja* entails the means for accumulating merit as well as the means for eliminating obscurations and unwholesome imprints.

### One's Spiritual Mentor as the Object of Devotion

There are many reason for choosing one's spiritual mentor as the object of devotion in the Seven-Limb Pūja. The primary reason is the very close connection one has with a mentor and the swiftness with which one can receive his or her blessing. The great Kargyüpa lama* Ku-tsam-pa said that among all the many objects of devotion there is none superior to one's own spiritual mentor.

It is also true that in the highest yoga tantra,* in the stages of generation and completion, there are many meditation deities upon whom one might focus and to whom one might make devotions, but none is higher than one's spiritual mentor.

Last but not least, it is said that one's spiritual mentor is the vehicle or instrument for the enlightened activities of all awakened beings. With this in mind, it is very powerful to direct one's devotion, both for the accumulation of merit as well as for purification, upon one's primary lama.

### Refuge and the Cultivation of Bodhicitta

When taking refuge and cultivating bodhicitta it is very potent to focus upon your spiritual mentor. Let it be his or her form you actually bring to mind, the lama in whom you have the greatest faith. You may have received teachings from many other teachers, other masters. Imagine them all being of the same nature as your own primary lama. Then imagine this lama as being of the nature of the entire Triple Gem: Buddha, Dharma and Sangha.

One approach is simply to visualize a single being, imagin-

ing all of the Triple Gem and all of the buddhas of the ten
directions included in the nature of that being. It is said that
if one focuses in this way on one's own spiritual mentor, and
then engages in offerings, prostrations, etc., one accrues the
same merit one would by the same devotions to all the buddhas.

Another approach is to visualize your primary lama sur-
rounded by your other teachers, and around them the buddhas,
bodhisattvas, the meditation deities, the guardians, the ḍākas
and ḍākinīs filling the whole of space. Once again, think of
them as being of the nature of all the buddhas of the three
times and the ten directions.

Try the different approaches and choose the one that is most
comfortable for you.

### The First Limb: Homage

The act of prostration is often mistaken by Westerners as
a degrading act of submission. On the contrary, it is an act
of humility, a quality most of us would do well to develop.
By prostrating three times before the Buddha and all awakened
beings, one surrenders to nature, to a force greater than oneself. It is an act that denotes the acceptance of one's dependent relationship to every aspect of existence.

### The Second Limb: Offerings

There are two kinds of offerings—actual and mental. Actual offerings include water bowls, candles, incense, flowers,
food, etc. Mental offerings have no limit. You can offer anything of beauty, anything you find attractive, such as leaves,
forests, mountains, the stars, the sun, the moon—you can even
offer your favorite department store and everything in it. The
list of possibilities is limited only by the imagination.

In addition to these formal offerings within the practice, we
can imagine offering everything we eat and drink to our
spiritual mentor and all the buddhas.

### The Third Limb: Confession

This aspect of the pūja contains three parts.

The first is the recognition and disclosure of unwholesome deeds, the breeches of any precepts, vows or commitments one has made in the past; and more specifically, any unwholesome imprints of harmful actions that might act as obstacles to the cultivation of śamatha. The second is developing a true feeling of remorse for having engaged in whatever act has been disclosed. The third is the generation of a firm resolve to avoid that kind of activity in the future.

In actuality, this three-step process goes beyond confession. It becomes an act of entrusting and surrendering oneself to the object of refuge—the Triple Gem.

*The Fourth Limb: Rejoicing*

Rejoicing simply means "taking delight in" or "being happy about" something. It is an extremely powerful practice, a supreme kind of devotion. It entails rejoicing in the wholesome activities of others—virtuous deeds, spiritual practices, devotions, meditation, etc. It entails rejoicing in the prosperity, happiness, and good fortune others encounter. They may have a beautiful or handsome form, they may be affluent, or successful. We can rejoice in this, recognizing that any good fortune itself arises as a result of virtue and wholesome actions. In addition, you can rejoice in the causes, the effects, and the wholesome deeds of awakened beings of the past, present and future, as well as your own virtuous deeds of the past and the present.

*The Fifth Limb: Requesting that the Dharma be Revealed*

Thinking of the darkness, the bewilderment and confusion of all sentient beings, as well as our own blindness in terms of what is to be adopted, practiced or avoided, beseech the awakened beings to reveal the Dharma. In making this request, one can go to one's spiritual mentor, or if you are using the more elaborate visualization, ask all the buddhas and bodhisattvas to turn the wheel of Dharma.

*The Sixth Limb: Requesting the Awakened Beings to Remain*

This request involves beseeching one's spiritual mentor and all awakened beings to continue teaching the Dharma in their present lives. In addition, one asks them to take rebirth in a form that will allow them to continue teaching just as long as there are confused and bewildered beings in need of their help.

*The Seventh Limb: Prayer of Supplication*

Finally, one asks to be liberated from all physical and mental conditions that might obstruct the cultivation of śamatha. In making this supplication to one's spiritual mentor, one should think, "May the unmistaken realization of śamatha swiftly arise on the stream (continuum) of my being." It is important to request "unmistaken realization" to insure that you not err in identifying your own experience.

In making this supplication it is also important to regard your spiritual mentor as being indivisible with, or of the same nature as, your meditation deity, the one with whom you have the strongest sense of connection. If you don't have a meditation deity that stands out from all the rest, then it is very helpful to focus on Mañjuśrī as the meditation deity, especially for the swift arising of insight. Because of his special motivation and prayers, Mañjuśrī is uniquely effective in this regard. If you feel as though you are about to be crushed by some kind of obstacle or problem, then it is of benefit to focus on Vajrapāṇi or Tārā because of their special motivation and prayer.

These general practices act as causes for the attainment of śamatha, and it is important to engage in them conscientiously from the very beginning. Initially they may not seem very important. However, neglecting them or treating them casually, even though it may not be evident in the beginning, will lead to obstacles or some kind of tangential path which will not lead to the development of meditative quiescence.

## BUILDING A STRONG FOUNDATION

The basic conditions necessary for the cultivation of śamatha entail both outer and inner causes. As we learn about them, it is important to recognize whether or not we already have them. If we do, the appropriate response is to try to strengthen and cultivate them. If we find that we are lacking in some of the causes, then it is crucial to acquire them as swiftly as possible. If, upon examination, we find that we are replete with all the necessary causes and conditions for cultivating śamatha and engaging properly in the practice, then it is simply a question of time and patience.

If we return to the analogy of the seed and the sprout, we see that if even one essential component is missing or flawed, the plant is doomed. If the water is poisoned or the earth is devoid of nutrients, no matter what the gardener does or how long he waits nothing will grow. But if all the necessary components are there in the right proportions and conditions—the seed, the earth, the water, the fertilizer, etc.—it just takes time for the plant to grow. Excessive effort will not make the plant grow faster. Now, the gardener has to sit back and let it happen—just let it happen. The same is true in meditation. If you have collected the appropriate conditions, the inevitable result will come in time.

## PATIENCE

Even in the beginning stages one might become impatient, thinking, "I really want to get this done quickly." One might think that by exerting more effort, by adding more and more stuff, by changing things this way or that way the process can be made to go faster. The good gardener knows that too much water or fertilizer is harmful, not helpful. The mature meditator must understand this as well. The Kadampa masters of old gave this counsel: First, pay great heed to getting the proper causes and conditions together. Next, engage in the practice without agitation and without anxiety. Then, with the mind at ease, carry on to the end.

## PHYSICAL AND MENTAL OBSTACLES

During the course of the retreat, physical or mental distress may arise or a strong obstacle will come up. When they do, don't try to ignore them. Don't try to bulldoze your way through them with sheer perseverance. The proper response is to stop the session, to deal with the obstacle, and dispel it. If you find that even minor obstacles or unfavorable circumstances, either inner or outer, are arising repeatedly for two or three days, go to your spiritual mentor for help.

If you deal with it quickly, it will probably not be a big deal and will be easily dispelled by following the advice of your mentor. And though it may seem a little simple-minded even to mention it, remember to listen to the advice that is given. Too often people have been given sound advice from deeper experience, but didn't listen to what was offered. As a result, they wound up with obstacles that need not have arisen, and had to scramble their way out of them.

## POTENTIAL PROBLEMS

In our current situation we are bound to hear noises from our neighbors and from the outside world. From the very outset of the practice, when this kind of sound occurs, do not identify with it. Do not become conceptually involved with it. *This is a very important point.* If you do identify with noise it can get to be a habit and will really damage your practice. So, when you hear noise, just let it pass. Do not become engrossed in it. Do not conceptually elaborate on it. Do not identify with it. Simply hear it, release it, and immediately go back to your practice and the object of meditation. If you follow this route, you will find that in the course of time you will not hear most noises at all. Noise will cease to be an issue.

Attitudes can be harmful too. There are two that are especially dangerous and detrimental to the practice. One is getting excited and thinking, "Oh, what a wonderful person I will be when I attain śamatha." The other is, "I bet I am better than other meditators. I'm going faster than they are. I'm going to get it and they aren't." These are easy traps to fall into. Be diligent in guarding against them.

It is very important to maintain clarity* of mind as a matter of course throughout the day. Getting sleepy during a number of sessions a day, as well as entering the meditation session with a drowsy or sluggish mind, can be either a nuisance or a serious problem. Sleepiness* must be remedied without delay.

It could simply be that you are drowsy because you are not getting enough sleep. The first and most obvious remedy for that is to go to bed earlier. If that doesn't cure the problem quickly it is important to find the cause and act to eliminate it quickly. An imbalance in the subtle energies in your body can lead to insomnia and damage meditation sessions the following day. There are a couple of very simple remedies for avoiding such insomnia. Rub some tiger balm, butter, or oil into your temples. Dress warmly when you go to bed and use sufficient blankets and heat. If these don't give you a good night's sleep, perhaps you might need to alter your diet by taking in more oils or fat, both of which help diminish *pranic* disturbances.* Also be sure to dress warmly during the day. If none of these antidotes work and if the problem begins to occur with some regularity, then by all means see your mentor for help.

At all times, both during and between meditation sessions, it is extremely important to maintain an appropriate balance between the tension of holding and the softness of relaxation. Try not to be too lax or too tight. Forcing, either to maintain too severe a discipline between sessions or holding the object of meditation too tightly, will obstruct any kind of realization or attainment. At the same time, too much relaxation will be a waste of time.

It is virtually certain that as the śamatha practice develops, certain types of visions or images will appear to the mind. When they do arise, whether they appear to be helpful or harmful, do not identify with them. Do not become engrossed with them. Do not elaborate on them. If they appear to be good visions, don't think, "Oh! This is tremendously auspicious." If they appear to be negative images, do not be depressed. Simply let them be, and maintain the object of your awareness.

Throughout the practice it is important to cultivate a sense of equanimity and acceptance. If you find some meditation sessions going well and concentration is good, do not respond with great satisfaction. As soon as the "Oh boy! This sure is a good session" attitude arises it will immediately halt whatever good is happening. If on the other hand, meditations go badly, if your concentration was bouncing all over the place, do not be depressed. Accept what seem to be good and bad sessions as a natural and inevitable aspect of the practice, and maintain equanimity.

## QUESTIONS AND ANSWERS

**Q:** Can you explain what you mean when you say that between sessions one should be neither too lax nor too tight?

**A:** Being too tight, too constrained, too withdrawn between sessions, is trying to maintain pretty close to the same quality of awareness between sessions as you had during the sessions, keeping the mind very focused, the eyes down, the mind really close, watching for the appearance of distracting thoughts. This is too tough. It will create problems in the body and mind.

Let the mind out a little between sessions. You have already brought it in. Now, let it gaze out. Don't look into other people's eyes or get involved in what you might see others doing. Look out at the horizon, at the mountains, at the sky. Anything with a little distance will help.

One extreme is trying to keep a strict meditative awareness during your breaks. That is too tight. The other extreme is losing yourself in a variety of activities, scurrying about, doing this and that. That is too loose—it will lead you into conceptualization and that will rob you of the calm you attained during the session. Balance yourself between the two. Let the mind come into a relaxed state, one in which you do not engross yourself in some kind of activity that captures the mind, agitates it, gets it strung out.

**Q:** I like to listen to tapes between sessions but I find that my mind becomes involved in what I hear. Is that too much to do during the break?

**A:** The great treatises on śamatha say that between sessions one should look into the practice in order to gain greater clarity and to see what qualms arise from your practice. So, the appropriate thing to do between sessions is to seek out those activities that create greater clarity. That is what is traditionally taught. Most important, see how every action affects your mind. If it causes agitation, stop. If it creates clarity and calm, go ahead and do it.

**Q:** In choosing the lama as the object for the Seven-Limb Pūja, you said to choose the lama that one has the most faith in. I am wondering, is there a difference in the use of the word *faith?* Does it have a different meaning? I found that difficult because when I went to do that, I found equal faith in all my lamas. Between His Holiness the Dalai Lama, and you, and all my other lamas, I could not find the "most faith."

**A:** This is a good place to be. In that case, since His Holiness is one of your teachers, then I suggest you focus on him.

For those who have been practicing for a while, it really begins to seem that all one's spiritual mentors, all one's lamas, are of the same nature. It really seems that they have just one mind. Maybe you meet a certain lama only very rarely, maybe once a year, and when you meet him he is very very happy and in a good mood. Then it seems that all of your lamas are in a good mood. When you meet other lamas after that it carries over to them too. Sometimes in dreams the different lamas are almost interchangeable. You may dream that you are on your way to meet Geshe Ngawang Dhargye, and then when you come to his house, His Holiness is there. They kind of pop in and out. As our obscurations are more and more purified, eventually we will see our own spiritual mentor, our own lama, as a supreme Nirmāṇakāya,* in other words, having the full thirty-two major and eighty minor marks, regardless of the attainment from his or her own side. When we have attained that level, then even if he or she is in hell, we will see our lama as a supreme Nirmāṇakāya.

**Q:** You said to imagine our mentors of the same nature as our meditation deities. I'm not exactly sure when this process comes into play. Is this in the guru devotion, or at some other point in the practice?

**A:** Whenever you are doing the devotional practices, be they at the beginning of each session, or between sessions, the Seven-Limb Pūja, or taking refuge, or any other, in any of these occasions, use this technique. Always bring the guru to mind and then imagine him or her to be of the same nature as the meditation deity.

For those of you who already have the practice of the Six-Session Guru Yoga, integrating the guru yoga into the śamatha practice, combining the two, makes the śamatha practice all the more effective. It will also aid your Six-Session Guru Yoga practice as well.

**Q:** Can you say something more about practices between sessions?

**A:** As far as one has commitments, recitations and prayers, those should be done between sessions. However, *the most important practice between sessions is to restrain the sense doors.* On one hand, regard the appearances of the senses as being symbols, manifestations, emanations of ultimate reality. In terms of the actual qualities of the different sensory appearances, there will be those that are attractive, unattractive and neutral. A natural tendency is to respond to attractive ones with attachment. If that happens, be on guard against attachment and apply antidotes. A natural tendency towards the unattractive is aversion, anger and aggression. If such aversion arises, apply antidotes to unhappiness and dissatisfaction. To neutral appearances, unspecified or neutral responses will arise. In that case one need do nothing at all.

If you are so inclined, it would be good to peruse contemplative written material, books on śamatha, in order to clarify your understanding. If you find during the course of the meditation sessions that you have a strong tendency towards excitement and agitation, then between sessions it is appropriate to reflect on subjects that give rise to renunciation—subjects such as the sufferings of cyclic existence or impermanence. In that case, it is also conducive to be reading such material. The important thing is to give rise to renunciation. That sobers the mind if you get excited.

On the other hand if you find that you are subject to drowsiness, sluggishness or laxity during the sessions, then between sessions it is appropriate to reflect in ways that arouse the mind: topics such as the preciousness and rarity of human life, bodhicitta, the advantages of developing śamatha and attaining liberation.

**Q:** When we are eating, bathing, doing laundry, that sort of thing, should we still be with the breath, or the Buddha image or whatever our object of meditation might be, or should we just try to keep general mindfulness?

**A:** The great treatises on śamatha suggest that even between sessions one ought to try to maintain some awareness of the main object of meditation. They do say, though, that one must be very careful about the intensity of that concentration. It is a balancing act, because if you do that too much you will become exhausted, and then you undermine your own practice. It is good to be somewhat aware of the object intermittently and then you can see how it affects you. Choose a level of attention according to your ability, without exhausting yourself. It is most important that you make sure you are getting refreshed and relaxed between sessions. Besides that, when you are eating, etc., there are different types of attitudes you might employ more actively: simply being aware of taste, and so forth—as if engaging in the Sūtrayāna* practice, thinking, "Now I take this food for sustenance of the body, to enable me to practice more effectively," etc.

If you are approaching the practice in a tantric context, then you can be transforming food into ambrosia. Generally speaking, in whatever activities you might be engaging in between sessions, mindfulness* should be there in a discriminating sense, making sure that the activities are of a wholesome nature. You always have the choice of more general or specific types of practice, and the balance must be an ongoing thing. You should be checking frequently to see what is appropriate and to be sure the balance is there.

Both mindfulness and discriminative alertness are needed in responding to sensory input of the three types—attractive, unattractive and neutral. Once again, in this tradition mindfulness does not mean simply to witness. It is a more discriminative kind of thing. You are asking yourself, "What is my response?" and then actively responding by applying the antidotes to attachment and hostility. The word *mindfulness* is a little bit different in different contexts. Here, mindfulness refers to the mental faculty of being able to maintain continuity of awareness of an object. *Vigilance** is concerned with the quality of mind, watching to see, for example, if the mind is veering off to other objects.

**PART II**
**THE COLLECTION OF
CAUSES FOR THE
CULTIVATION OF
ŚAMATHA**

# 3   The Six Essential Causes

## 1. DWELLING IN A FAVORABLE ENVIRONMENT

For a perfectionist, it could be very difficult to fulfill all the requirements just as they are described in the scriptures, but we can come close.

> —A peaceful environment, in the sense that during the day there is not a lot of human commotion and during the night there is little noise, barking of dogs, etc.
> —The land, the earth itself, is a good place. The best location would be a place where great meditators have lived before and left their positive energy.
> —The necessities of life, such as food, water, etc., are provided or easily available.
> —A good human environment, good companions who hold similar views and are engaged in a similar practice.

"Holding similar views" simply means having similar attitudes. "Similar practice" refers to the behavior of the three doors (the body, speech and mind)—that they are in accord with one's own. This accord can either be natural, or it can come about through some effort.

Here in this current situation, we come about as close as anyone possibly could to having collected the necessary causes. We are living in a beautiful, friendly, secluded forest, and all the necessities of life are being provided by a wonderful support staff. The two points of similar attitude and similar view are also essentially satisfied. We do have a common aspiration in the nature of our practice, and in the nature of our behavior there is a fair degree of accord among the people here. What we must do now is try to be considerate and help each other whenever we can by being silent and unintrusive.

## 2 & 3. REDUCING DESIRES AND DEVELOPING CONTENTMENT

These two causes refer to abandoning or setting aside one's mundane concerns for this life alone and totally dedicating oneself to the attainment of full awakening. In Tsong-kha-pa's explanation, having few desires refers to not wishing for something better than what you already have in terms of lodging, clothes, food, etc. It means not fantasizing that "it would be better this way or that." Desires of that nature will bring about more activity of body and speech, which will act as an obstacle to meditation.

The other side of the coin is contentment, the third of the six causes. It is focused upon present reality, simply being satisfied with what is adequate. If one lacks this contentment, then this too gives birth to various types of activity, both verbal and physical, which then clutter the practice. The point to be emphasized here is that contentment helps us avoid the clutter.

These problems seem to be more prevalent if one is living in isolation, in some remote retreat hut where you are totally on your own. Here where we can write a note and ask the staff to provide the things we feel we need, it should be less of a problem. We also have a structure here, a one-year retreat. This should tend to reduce some of the clutter of the mind.

The special danger we do face is anticipating the end of the retreat and thinking about the desires we will have then, the hamburgers and ice cream we can have then, the luxurious living conditions to which we will return. The temptation will be to borrow distractions from a year hence and take advantage of them right now. Westerners are so clever, they can think of things way, way in advance. Unfortunately, planning ahead may not be appropriate now. The Abhidharma* calls desiring things that you do not have now "having great desire" which is the exact opposite of contentment. All of this refers to things of a mundane nature. Discontent comes into sharp focus when you think, "This is not satisfactory." The antidote for such discontentment is to look at what you have and say, "This suffices."

## 4. REJECTING A MULTITUDE OF ACTIVITIES

This is relatively clear. In general, during a retreat, a wide variety of activities should be avoided. One should not engage in business transactions of any kind. It is extremely important for ordained as well as non-ordained practitioners not to have a lot of personal contact with other people, no social activities. This isn't a very complicated topic. We can see from experience that when we have a lot of interpersonal contact it tends either to elate the mind or to depress it. This kind of upset of the mind is a major obstacle to śamatha. Watch carefully to see if any of your activities are superfluous and avoid them.

## ✓ 5. MAINTAINING PURE MORAL DISCIPLINE

One should abide in pure moral discipline. This means avoiding activities that are proscribed, i.e., prohibited in general, as well as maintaining precepts specific to those who have taken vows. On both counts, these are to be guarded very carefully. If, on occasion, one breaks any one of the precepts, restore it through proper purification practices.

Activities that are proscribed are just as unwholesome for

those who have not taken vows as for those who have. Those activities deemed unwholesome regardless of who does them are chiefly activities of speech and body. The other type of misdeed, or downfall, is proscribed for those who have taken precepts—this can refer to monastic precepts as well as bodhisattva* and tantric precepts.

For example, the ten non-virtuous deeds of killing, stealing, etc., are unwholesome regardless of whether or not one has taken precepts. All of us have committed some of these actions in this lifetime and certainly in previous lifetimes. So, it is to our advantage to confess or disclose any such non-virtuous actions as an aid to our śamatha practice. In that the bodhisattva and tantric vows are taken voluntarily, their transgression falls into a second category.

In the context of Buddhist practices there are a number of methods that are designed to purify the unwholesome imprints of non-virtuous actions. Others are designed to prevent the imprints of unwholesome actions from increasing, which they will naturally do if left unpurified. One example is the Vajrasattva practice with the visualization and mantra.* If one recites the mantra with the full practice twenty-one times a day, it is said that this will prevent unwholesome imprints from increasing in power from day to day. Therefore, it is good to make this a daily practice, something that can easily be done between sessions. Recite the mantra twenty-one times along with the whole meditation, followed by the four remedial powers.*

There are other practices such as the prayer to the thirty-five buddhas, the dedication of merit and prostrations. All can be utilized in order to prevent unwholesome seeds from increasing. However, if one is not familiar with these practices, they are all included in the Vajrasattva practice, which suffices.

It would be best for those who have taken commitments in terms of daily practices of a tantric nature to maintain them. If we let them slack off, we will be committing an infraction. Later on, when our concentration gets very strong, very stable, as time is growing short and we are squeezed for doing all those commitments, there are ways they can be altered or abbreviated with no problem. For the time being, however, do them completely. If you abbreviate them at the beginning and do not attain śamatha, then you lose on both accounts.

## 6. REJECTING THOUGHTS OF DESIRE FOR SENSUAL OBJECTS

The desires included at this juncture are those entailed in the eight worldly dharmas.* As I mentioned earlier, if one's motivation for the cultivation of śamatha is the fulfillment of one's wishes just for this life, it falls into this category. If one aspires to attain śamatha thinking of the great reputation or financial gain one can acquire, or thinking that through the attainment of śamatha one will be able to buy a bigger and better wardrobe or a new gourmet kitchen, all that falls into this category and will be an unfavorable motivation.

Here is the essential point: The mind that attains śamatha is a mind that has gained access concentration to the first dhyana, which is included in the form realm. The form realm lies beyond the sensual realm. Therefore, if one's very aspiration is clinging to something that is of the sensual realm, the motivation for the practice acts as an obstacle to the fulfillment of that aspiration. It is internally inconsistent.

# 4 Cultivating Śamatha in Dependence upon the Essential Causes

## PREPARATION

The preliminary practices we have already discussed—refuge, cultivation of bodhicitta and the Seven-Limb Pūja—suffice as preparations for the actual practice. In the Seven-Limb Pūja, even if one does not do all of the seven limbs, the most important are confession (the disclosure of unwholesome deeds), rejoicing in virtue (of others as well as one's own), and the dedication of merit including the offering of prayers.

The Six-Session Guru Yoga, if that is already part of your practice, is also a means of daily preparation for practice. The most effective way of approaching it is to do three sessions during the daylight hours and three during the dark hours after sunset and before dawn. Do not do the morning and evening prayers all together. Do each session separately either at the beginning of meditation sessions or between them.

The cultivation of bodhicitta as a basis of motivation at the beginning of each session, and the dedication of merit at the end can be done in an abbreviated way for many sessions through the day. However, give special attention to the cultivation of bodhicitta during your first session in the morning and more particular concern to the dedication of merit at the end of your last session in the evening. Focus especially on these two practices, on renunciation and great compassion. Whether or not one's practice is effective in leading toward the attainment of full awakening depends on the foundation of pure motivation. That is why the cultivation of motivation is so strongly emphasized. The important thing is not that one actually cultivate fully perfected bodhicitta, or fully perfected loving kindness. Even an approximation of bodhicitta or loving kindness for the benefit of all beings will accrue great merit. That great merit will then act as a very favorable circumstance and be helpful in the cultivation of śamatha. Insofar as we can cultivate loving kindness, compassion and bodhicitta focused on all sentient beings, then just as the number of all beings is limitless and as vast as space, so then do we acquire merit corresponding to their vastness.

On the other hand, if we engage in even very deep practices without that foundation of motivation the merit accrued is comparatively very little. The *Essence of the Middle Way* tells us to cultivate altruism over an extended period of time. Even if one does not have a great sense of it to begin with, the very act of cultivation, that very concern for the welfare of others is, itself, a service to others.

## THE ACTUAL PRACTICE

### Posture and Other Physical Aspects

In general, it is said that the supreme posture for meditative quiescence is the full lotus posture. There are many auspicious ramifications of using it, but it is a difficult posture to maintain. If it is very uncomfortable, the half lotus will do, as will the ordinary cross-legged position which is called the bodhisattva posture. Use the one you find most comfortable.

Place the hands in the lap, the left hand beneath the right and the thumbs touching lightly. When the meditation is going well, you might find that the thumbs will start pressing together with force, and this can cause some pain in the joints. If such pain arises the mind is disturbed. In general, the hands should be very relaxed. You can help keep your thumbs touching lightly and your hands soft by placing something soft under them as a gentle support. A small pillow or even just a fold in your meditation blanket should be sufficient.

The spine should be perfectly straight and upright. Normally, there is a slight curve in the upper back. In meditation we try to straighten that curve out. The proper position for the head is slightly tilted or inclined to the front with the chin tucked back toward the neck. As you straighten the curve in the back, it is important to keep the head from falling back. Conversely, when you tilt the head forward the tendency is to let it fall all the way forward. That too is a problem.

The eyes should be slightly open. If the position of the head is correct, the eyes will then focus gently and unforced on the floor about three feet in front of you.

Keep the jaw and lips soft. Let the tongue rest gently against the palate just behind your teeth. This position helps keep the saliva in the mouth when the mind becomes rather stable and there is a tendency to drool.

There is an almost irresistible tendency to elevate the shoulders. Don't. Let them relax. Let them drop down.

It is important that your cushion be exactly level, not tilted to either side. If there is an incline to the left or right, to the front or the rear, it's going to cause problems. They may not be so evident during the beginning stages of the meditation. You may find yourself saying, "Ah. This hardly matters." After awhile, as meditation becomes deeper, the only way you'll know the problem has arrived is when you start to keel over to one side. You can test the level of your cushion by placing a bowl of water on it, checking to see if the liquid tilts to one side or the other.

Don't let your posture become too tight. Let the body be very relaxed, very natural. If you get tight in certain areas, take a deep breath and then exhale the tension with the next out-breath. In the course of time, wherever there is too much tightness, tension will arise there and you will feel pain and discomfort. That will act as an obstacle to your practice. If you develop bad habits in the first two or three months, it will take another two or three months to break them.

Be conscientious about maintaining good posture right from the beginning. In the first ten to fifteen days of your retreat, be especially watchful of your posture. When you feel even the slightest presence of tension, do whatever is necessary to correct the situation.

Pay special attention to the coccyx. There is a natural tendency to let it roll forward a bit. If that happens over a long period of time it will cause problems all over the body. Tuck the pelvis forward and think of the coccyx as an arrow pointing into the earth. If you are having trouble keeping the pelvis tilted in the proper manner, keeping the arrow pointing down, find something to support it. You can use a small pillow or even a folded towel will do. Don't sit on the support. Just nudge it right up there at the base of the spine. This will help you hold the bottom of the spine perfectly erect.

Sitting erect with a straight back creates the least stress on the body and one is able to sit for long periods of time without feelings of pain or exhaustion. Another advantage of the erect posture is that the channels within the body are not scrunched up. They're nice and straight, they are free and the energies within them are free to flow more easily. Because of the very close relationship between the mind, the states of consciousness and the *prana*,* a smooth, uninterrupted flow of prana enhances both the clarity as well as the stability of the mind. Slouching over yields laxity, mental sluggishness, drowsiness, and eventually sleep. The erect posture gives rise to vitality and enhanced awareness.

Erect posture is highly conducive to the arising of two forms of pliancy.* Physical pliancy is a supple sensation one feels in the body, a very pleasurable tactile sensation associated with the movement of the subtle energies of prana within the body. Mental pliancy is an actual mental event which renders the body and mind "fit for action" or "serviceable."

The function of pliancy is the eradication of obscurations. Moreover, both mental and physical pliancy act as an antidote for dysfunction* which is the opposite of serviceability.*

Pliancy is a direct antidote for dysfunction, as well as a remedy for what are sometimes called the five faults. Beyond that, pliancy acts as an antidote for both afflictive and cognitive obscurations.

As the body and mind become more and more stable, mental pliancy arises quite naturally, without any forceful effort. It is a mental state accompanied by immense joy. Physical pliancy follows quickly. The body is truly "serviceable"; it takes on a suppleness that enables one to assume any posture and sit for hours and hours without feeling the slightest fatigue.

Actually, all of us are endowed with both mental and physical pliancy, but it is not in a manifest state. When conditions are ripe and they actually do manifest, the joy that accompanies this blissful state increases to a peak and then tapers off. After this tapering off there arises a more stable, non-fluctuating kind of subtle pliancy which is the most effective.

*Counting the Breath*

Sitting in the proper posture, one can engage in this introductory practice. Following the breath in and out, one may count up to seven or twenty-one. Most important is seeing how much of the conceptual mind has been quieted by this technique. If that mind is still rambunctious even after a series of twenty-one breaths, continue counting from one again. If the conceptual mind is quiet after just seven breaths, the introductory practice of counting breath has served its function. There is no need to go on. This is pertinent to all śamatha techniques.

## QUESTIONS AND ANSWERS

**Q:** My eyes keep wanting to close. Is it absolutely necessary to keep them open during meditation?

**A:** Keeping the eyes just slightly open during meditation can be very helpful for clarity of the mind. Closing your eyes seems easier in the beginning because there is no visual distraction. In the long run, however, it is a disadvantage. It makes it harder to develop clarity, real vividness of mind. Keeping the eyes open also helps counteract lethargy.*

As difficult as it may seem right now, keep working on it and see if you can ease into it slowly.

**Q:** Which cushion are you referring to when you say it should be level?

**A:** It's the zabuton that should be flat. As for the zafu, Tibetans don't use them so there is no thousand-year tradition. My feeling is that it would probably be best to sit on the front edge of the zafu. It should give you a more grounded feeling. The most important thing is to check for yourself. The effects will become apparent.

**PART III**
**CULTIVATING**
**FAULTLESS**
**SAMĀDHI**

# 5 How to Perform Prior to Directing the Mind to the Object of Meditation

This subject entails a discussion based upon a text by Maitreya, *The Examination of the Center and the Extremes,* which elaborates on the five faults that act as obstacles to attainment, and the eight antidotes to those faults that aid one in focusing the mind properly on the object.

| THE FIVE FAULTS AND EIGHT ANTIDOTES | |
|---|---|
| **The Five Faults** | **The Eight Antidotes** |
| | Pliancy |
| Laziness | Enthusiasm |
| | Aspiration |
| | Faith |
| Forgetfulness | Mindfulness |
| Laxity and Excitement | Vigilance |
| Non-application | Application |
| Application | Equanimity |

## THE FIRST FAULT: LAZINESS

Laziness* is a mental factor identified as a lack of delight in the wholesome, the virtuous. This is its aspect. Its function is to distract one from wholesome activity. Laziness is attached to sloth and does not delight in virtue. It is often attached to various types of entertainments, such as movies, television, theater, music, etc.

There are three types of laziness:

a) The laziness that is attracted to bad actions, in this particular case the things that turn one away from the practice of śamatha. It manifests itself as indulgence in other kinds of activity.

b) The laziness of sloth is frequently identified with procrastination. Under its influence, one thinks, "It really would be good to meditate, but not quite yet. I think I'll take a nap." Those who suffer from this form of laziness are attached to lying around.

c) The last type of laziness is self-denigrating laziness. You will know you are suffering from it when you put yourself down by thinking, "I couldn't do it even if I tried. Why bother?"

In this context, the nature of laziness is not being attracted to or interested in the cultivation of concentration, but being interested in and attracted to other activities. It acts as a serious obstacle to entering into the practice of concentration. For practice in progress, it acts as an obstacle to the continuation of that practice by interrupting its continuity.


## FOUR ANTIDOTES TO LAZINESS

*Pliancy*

This is the first and most direct antidote to laziness; however, it comes into full play only when the practice reaches advanced stages. The joy that is born in pliancy brings an immediate end to laziness. For those who have attained śamatha, it is a tremendous boon for cultivating the succeeding stages on the path to awakening.

This does not mean that you should forget about it now because it comes to its full bloom only after you attain śamatha. There are many stages to the practice. Pliancy comes in brief flashes in the beginning. As the practice matures, the flashes become moments; the moments become seconds; the seconds become minutes; and on it goes. Practicing śamatha is like sharpening the blade of an axe. It is not accomplished with a single stroke.

You sharpen the axe so you can cut down a tree. If you don't cut it down, you've wasted your time. In similar fashion, you practice śamatha in order to cultivate the subsequent stages of the path. If you attain śamatha and fail to take that next step, you have expended your time and energy for nothing.

How does one cultivate pliancy?

### Enthusiasm

This is a mental factor which delights in virtue. That is its aspect. It is the means by which we cultivate pliancy.

The function of enthusiasm* is that it brings about various insights along the path to awakening. Enthusiasm is also defined as a state of happiness, something that delights in virtue. The persevering cultivation of enthusiasm yields as its result the attainment of pliancy, which is, in its turn, the direct antidote to laziness.

How does one cultivate enthusiasm?

### Aspiration

In this context aspiration* refers to a wholesome wish for attainment and realization, not just any kind of base desire. It is through this wholesome aspiration that enthusiasm is cultivated.

How does one cultivate aspiration?

### Faith

The cause of faith* in śamatha is a mind that clearly recalls the virtues and benefits of mental quiescence. That mind is marked by the aspect of faith.

There are three types of faith:

a)  Faith of belief
b)  Lucid faith
c)  Faith of an active aspiration

The faith referred to here includes all three. The faith of belief is fundamental to the other two. It entails the conviction that there is such a thing as śamatha, that it is attainable, that it does have the kinds of results that are described—heightened awareness, psychic powers, and far more important, the attainment of liberation and full awakening. All of these can be attained in dependence upon śamatha. Thus, that kind of conviction is the most fundamental type of faith. Lucid faith and the faith of aspiration evolve from this basic capital.

The truth of these statements—that there is such a thing as śamatha, that full awakening is possible in dependence upon śamatha—is the kind of truth that is concealed, not evident, not easily accessible, not something that we can ascertain immediately for ourselves. Although it is concealed, this is only temporary. Many have had their own experience of certain physical and mental bliss, many have experienced those states of being through their own practice, and many have the faith that those states suggest much deeper attainments.

States of being beyond our present experience—such as the attainment of heightened awareness, psychic powers, liberation, full awakening—are described to us by authentic teachers who are much further developed along the spiritual path than we are. We can take them at their word, or not. The choice is ours. If we don't believe, then we don't do the practice. If we do have faith and begin, the more we persist and continue in the practice of śamatha, more and more aspects of reality become apparent to the mind, and we experience deeper realities than we have ever known before.

The deeper we go, the more credence we will give to statements made by those who are yet further along the path and the firmer our faith will become. As we go more profoundly into the practice we will find from our own experience that the mind becomes more serene, more relaxed, more at ease. Joy, states of bliss and pliancy actually do arise. As they arise, faith arises and we are honestly able to tell ourselves, "This kind of thing exists and it's bound to improve."

We can even set aside the things that are quite beyond our current experience, things such as heightened awareness, psychic powers, etc. Just the deepening relaxation of the mind is enough of a base upon which we can begin to build a strong foundation of faith in the teachings of those many meditators who have experienced various types of increased awareness and serenity.

In this moment, as we begin our retreat, when many of us are excited and enthusiastic about the practice, it is a good idea to etch these points into our minds. As time passes, one or two months from now, the days will seem long, boredom will set in, and laziness is likely to arise. When that happens, think back to these points and you will find that you are generating your own internal motivation to get back into gear.

## THE INTERACTION OF THE FOUR ANTIDOTES

The four antidotes to laziness are interwoven into a tapestry of symbiotic dependency. Pliancy is indeed the primary antidote to laziness. How does one cultivate pliancy? By means of continually cultivating enthusiasm for the practice of concentration. What is the cause of enthusiasm? A very strong aspiration to cultivate concentration. How does one cultivate a very strong aspiration? By faith that sees the excellent qualities of developing meditative quiescence. Faith, in turn, is cultivated by the first stirrings of pliancy, and the circle goes around again, with every turn increasing the strength of each of the antidotes.

To draw a parallel, we can look at mundane experience: We see an object with excellent qualities and think we might like to acquire it. We ponder its excellence, reflect upon it, upon how good it would be to have the object, of how many uses it would have. Through this process, our faith in the quality of the object increases until our aspiration to acquire it arises effortlessly. Aspiration continues to arise until the enthusiasm to buy it sends us scurrying off to the store. Once we have bought it, we come home and use it. In this analogy, the object is pliancy.

The faith which is the foundation of the structure might be confused by some as attachment, and it is important to discern the difference between the two. To do so, we have to ask two questions. First: Is it possible to cultivate attachment for the attainment of śamatha? Second: If so, how would that be distinguished from yearning, the faith that inspires aspiration?

The answer to the first question is: Yes. It is possible to have an attachment to meditative quiescence. In this case there would first be an attachment to oneself. Then, upon that basis of self-directed attachment, one would think, "Oh, if I only had meditative quiescence, it would be so good for me. How grand that would be!" It would be like seeing śamatha as some kind of adornment, it would be indulgence in one's attachment to self. That is how attachment to the attainment of śamatha arises.

In contrast to that, the aspiration for the attainment of śamatha is not based upon attachment to self. It focuses on śamatha itself and recognizes its excellent qualities. It aspires to the attainment of the qualities, not the glory or the personal satisfaction that attachment seeks.

Attachment is a mental factor that focuses upon something that is contaminated, seeing it as attractive and then craving to acquire it.

Faith, in contrast, is something that arises as an antidote towards the lack of faith (i.e., faithlessness) and it also sees the excellent qualities of the object in question. In order to develop faith which is focused on śamatha, it is necessary to be aware of and familiar with the excellent qualities of śamatha.

## THE EXCELLENT QUALITIES OF ŚAMATHA

One of the excellent qualities of meditative quiescence is that upon its arising there occur both physical and mental pliancy. This brings about a tremendous state of physical and mental well-being which is called "visible joy" because it is something that you can experience in this very life. In dependence upon the joy of mental and physical pliancy experienced in this life, one's spiritual practice is greatly enhanced, and this is something of benefit in future lifetimes.

Moreover with the attainment of śamatha, mental distraction is pacified and because the compulsion for mental distraction is also pacified, one is far less prone to unwholesome behavior. Not only is one less likely to engage in unwholesome activities, but one's engagement in virtue is tremendously enhanced.

If one engages in a practice before the attainment of śamatha, in the cultivation of proper motivation there is a great deal of competition from all kinds of conceptual activity. One is bombarded, confused and congested with other conceptual processes right at the outset of the practice. During the course of the practice, because the mind is subject to distraction, to conceptual congestion, the virtuous practice will be diluted. Then upon the conclusion of the practice, as one seeks to dedicate the merit, again the mind is congested with other conceptualizations and the dedication gets diluted as well. So, for the whole course of the practice, from beginning to end, it is difficult for the practice to have the potency that it would if one had already attained śamatha.

When we arrive at the point of death, the determining factor for the type of birth we will take in the next life depends on whether our store of imprints from previous actions is predominantly wholesome or unwholesome. As a consequence of that predominance, one takes a more favorable or less favorable rebirth. If one has enhanced one's spiritual practice with the cultivation of meditative quiescence, which tremendously empowers one's engagement in wholesome activities, this will lead to a much greater store of wholesome imprints, which in turn will naturally lead to future favorable rebirths as well. The attainment of śamatha has long-term effects.

Moreover, upon the attainment of śamatha, it is possible to be completely focused upon ultimate truth while cultivating insight, and by means of attaining such insight it is possible to cut the root of the cycle of existence. By doing so, one is completely and irrevocably liberated from suffering. Beyond that, it is also possible to attain the full awakening of a buddha by engaging in appropriate practices with the single-pointed concentration of śamatha.

A true familiarity with the excellent qualities of śamatha will be very helpful to the practice in two specific ways. First, when laziness occasionally occurs, reflecting upon these points will act as a direct antidote. And second, in a case where laxity* arises, contemplation on the advantages of śamatha will arouse the mind and act as an antidote to laxity.

Above and beyond all the excellent qualities already described, it is said that in dependence upon the attainment of meditative quiescence, it is possible to attain various forms of heightened awareness, including clairvoyance and psychic powers. Upon the attainment of psychic powers you can dispense with mundane forms of transportation like cars and jets. You can also stop paying your phone bill and give away your radio too, because when one attains good clairaudience you can hear even very distant sounds. If your clairaudience is only moderately good, you can still hear everything within five hundred miles or so. You might think that could give you a real earache, but you won't have to be concerned that you might be flooded with sounds all the time. With that kind of clairaudience you have a built-in switch. You can turn it off or on any time you like.

QUESTIONS AND ANSWERS

**Q:** What is lucid faith?

**A:** Lucid faith is a deep appreciation in and of the heart.

Let's say there are three people. The first thinks, "Śamatha is nice but I'm not going to go for it." The second thinks, "Śamatha is really wonderful. It's more than wonderful. It's fantastic!" The third thinks, "Not only is it wonderful, I really do want to attain it!"

There is a definite sequence here that shows it is possible to have a belief without really appreciating it. The first person has belief and nothing more. "Big deal. Heightened awareness. Who cares?" That is one way. Then there is the person who believes śamatha is nice, a possibility, and who does nothing about it because, "It's not relevant to me. I want to make money." The third person has the belief, appreciation, and aspiration. The combination of the three is lucid faith. It is the faith that sees the advantages and benefits of the specific attainment, the faith which delights in the attainment.

Keep in mind that it is also possible simply to have attachment for the attainment. If there is delight rising out of attachment, that is not faith. That is attachment.

# 6 *Another Look at Bodhicitta*

Twenty-five hundred years ago, the Buddha Śākyamuni cultivated bodhicitta, developed the awakening mind, attained full
awakening, and turned the wheel of Dharma. If one looks upon
the results of the Buddha's bodhicitta, one sees that it has
brought about countless benefits, such as the attainments of
the eighty-four mahāsiddhas* of classical India, of sages and
contemplatives of all four orders of Tibetan Buddhism, as well
as the great flourishing of the Dharma in Mongolia, China,
India, Sri Lanka, Burma, and Thailand. Many beings have
attained the full awakening of a buddha. In dependence upon
his teachings, an inconceivable number of beings have attained
arhatship and gained liberation. They, in turn, have guided
countless others to liberation.

If one were to try to identify the number of beings who have
benefited by the Buddha's bodhicitta, it would be impossible. It is for this reason that it is said that bodhicitta is equal
to ambrosia, a life-giving nectar that dispels the suffering of
sentient beings. Thus, the motivation to attain the full awakening of a buddha for the benefit of all creatures, let alone the
actual arising of bodhicitta, is an extraordinary event.

For us, this is an opportunity first to cultivate a facsimile
of bodhicitta, and then to cultivate actual bodhicitta, an op-

portunity to proceed along the path of full awakening. It is a golden opportunity to develop bodhicitta to its culmination, a time when we can enact the Twelve Principal Deeds of a fully awakened being. It is even possible that we could be of direct benefit in this lifetime to even more beings than the Buddha Śākyamuni was. It would not be because our attainment was greater, but because when the Buddha lived he had access to a relatively few beings and many were not able to benefit from his teachings.

In this era, the opportunity we have before us right now to engage in spiritual practice is also an effect of the Buddha's own bodhicitta, of course. Therefore, it is meaningful for us to thoroughly cultivate bodhicitta as the motivation for our practice: "May I attain the full awakening of a buddha for the benefit of all creatures." Without giving it careful thought, when we say, "for the benefit of all sentient beings, may I attain buddhahood . . . ," it may seem very abstract, almost ridiculous. If we look into it more deeply we will be able to recognize the tremendous benefit that can arise from such a practice.

In his *Guide to the Bodhisattva's Way of Life,* Śantideva says that the chance of the jewel of bodhicitta arising in one's being is equal to the chance of a blind beggar finding the wish-fulfilling gem while rummaging about in a pile of garbage. To imagine a blind beggar finding the wish-fulfilling jewel in a pile of garbage is totally outrageous, seemingly outside the realm of possibility. Yet, if such a thing were to happen, imagine the joy with which the blind beggar would respond.

In terms of our ignorance, in terms of all the causes and conditions necessary for the cultivation and arising of bodhicitta, we can imagine ourselves as being like the blind beggar. The rubbish heap in which we rummage is the whole mass of unwholesome imprints we have accumulated. The point that Śantideva is making here is that it is equally outrageous and improbable that we would have this opportunity of being able to cultivate bodhicitta. Having recognized that such an immensely improbable event has, in fact, taken place, our appropriate response should be one of great joy and delight.

It is the same for śamatha. For all the diverse causes and conditions necessary for the practice to come together seems utterly impossible, and yet they have. Now, we can take these virtual impossibilities and combine them by cultivating bodhicitta as the very motivation for cultivating śamatha.

We have the immense good fortune to have attained a human rebirth, and within the human realm we have these practically impossible conditions of leisure and solitude in which to cultivate śamatha. Improbabilities and virtual impossibilities compounded have allowed for this magnificent opportunity. It is important to rejoice and take delight in this, especially when we encounter moments of discouragement. Think of yourself as the blind beggar who has found the jewel. This can arouse the mind, excite the mind to practice. It can act as an antidote to laziness and laxity.

# 7 *Directing the Mind to the Object During Meditation*

## ASCERTAINING THE SPECIFIC OBJECT OF MEDITATION

The breath is the object of meditation recommended for those who are strongly inclined to conceptualization or imagination. In the practice of śamatha there are four classifications of types of objects. The breath as an object is included in the one called objects of purification for specific types of behavior. Here, behavior refers to over-conceptualization. Breath is simply one among several objects that are included in a category that specifically refers to predilections that result from habitual behavior in previous lives. (Breath as an object is discussed in more detail later in this chapter.)

There is another object for those who have a strong predilection for attachment, and yet others for people dominated by other specific mental distortions. Those who have a low level of mental distortions, and those whose mental distortions are all about on the same level can choose anything they like.

For those who have a more or less even level of different mental distortions, there is a special purpose or benefit in focusing on the image of the Buddha. In fact, the Buddha as an object of meditation has many advantages. The development of stability in that visualization is useful for the practices of the accumulation of merit, for the purification of obscurations and unwholesome imprints. In addition, to be able to bring the Buddha image to mind at any moment is very useful. Finally, the Buddha as an image can be very useful for those who are doing or hoping to do tantric practices involving visualization.

## THE SECOND FAULT: FORGETFULNESS

The nature of forgetfulness* is that it comes under the influence of mental distortions and brings about a lack of clarity in terms of what is wholesome and virtuous. Its function is to obstruct the arising of concentration.

All these terms—mindfulness, vigilance, forgetfulness, and all the rest—have very precise meanings in the context of śamatha. These meanings are very different from the general meaning or those implied in other contexts.

In this context, forgetfulness means losing the object. When you are focusing on the object of meditation, as soon as you have lost it, forgetfulness has already arisen. This describes a much more precise and subtle type of event than is generally denoted by the term *forgetfulness.*

## ESTABLISHING THE FAULTLESS APPROACH

In order to establish the faultless approach, it is said that one needs to cultivate two properties of awareness. First, one's mind should be endowed with non-discursive stability.* Second, it should be endowed with a vigor, or strength of clarity.*

### Non-Discursive Stability

The manner of achieving this first required property is through mindfulness. To initiate that process, first of all there has to be an object of mindfulness with which one is already familiar. Mindfulness, then, entails a lack of forgetfulness. Its function is being free of mental distraction. It is the antidote to forgetfulness and, like forgetfulness, is a mental factor.

Concentration refers to a mental factor having the function of focusing continually upon a designated entity. Here, the expression "designated entity" refers to a mental image or object. If the breath is the object of meditation, it would also refer to a physical object. Elsewhere it will have a different meaning. Moreover, concentration has the function of yielding insight. This is a precise definition of the term *samādhi,** which acts as a basis for the arising of insight.

Keep in mind that what we are discussing here is the manner of directing the mind to the object. Within that framework, what does directing the mind to the object mean? It means to *apprehend*. Remember the term. It will come up again.

*Strength of Clarity*

The second of the two properties one needs to cultivate in establishing the faultless approach is vigor, or strength of clarity. The term *strength of clarity* means just what it says, that one just has great clarity. This does not refer to the clarity or lucidity of the object. It refers to the mode in which the mind apprehends the object. The distinction between the clarity of the object and the clarity of the mind is an extremely important one. If the mind is very vividly apprehending its object, strength of clarity is present.

We can draw an analogy with television. Sometimes the image on the screen will be hazy around the edges—it appears with a "ghost" image. In this case, the fuzzy image with the ghost would be lacking strength of clarity. If the mind of the viewer watching the screen is apprehending its object but going in and out of focus, if its mode of apprehension is hazy around the edges, then it is the mind that is lacking clarity. In this case, both the mind and the image lack clarity. If you have a really terrific thousand-dollar TV set with a perfectly sharp picture, and it is still apprehended by the mind as unfocused, then it is the mind that is lacking in clarity, not the object.

In the meditation practice, when the meditator lacks that strength of clarity of mind the object generally appears hazy. Generally, when one has strength of clarity of mind, the outlines of the object are very crisp.

## THE THIRD FAULT: LAXITY AND EXCITEMENT

What acts to deteriorate the strength of clarity? While the mind is focused on the object, it is laxity manifesting as lethargy* that causes the mind to retract or withdraw within itself rather than being right out there focusing sharply on its object.

If we examine our own experience in moments when we are consumed by very strong attachment—lust, anger, strong pride or conceit, jealousy—we can recognize that our minds are endowed with great strength of clarity when these mental distortions arise with great force. For example, when we direct great wrath towards another person, he or she appears in our mind with unusual lucidity and vividness. It is not the same as actually confronting another person face to face, nevertheless an almost lifelike image will appear in the mind with unusually sharp focus.

In higher practices such as tantra, not only does one not try to counteract or suppress attachment and anger, one transforms them into the path. In that way these mental distortions become a means through which one attains higher realization. How is it possible? It is possible because mental images and visualizations coming from attachment and anger have exceptional strength of clarity and appear vividly to the mind. Rather than trying to subdue them, one simply uses them.

The attainment of full awakening is reached by means of cultivating the path, and in order to cultivate the path, the objects of one's meditations must be vivid. Two elements are essential in order to produce that state of vividness: first, real vividness from the side of the object; and second, real strength of clarity from the side of the meditating mind.

When we engage in the cultivation of bodhicitta, renunciation, compassion or loving kindness, when cultivating a mind that wishes to arise from the cycle of existence and when reflecting on the virtues of our spiritual mentor, we are cultivating these qualities subjectively. For these, one must have strength of clarity from the side of the subject, from the side of the meditating mind. That clarity must arise from within our own being.

On the other hand for subjects such as emptiness and subtle impermanence it is necessary to have vividness from the side of the object. You want to have a very clear vision of emptiness or subtle impermanence arise from their side.

In essence, we are talking about two types of meditation. The Tibetan word translated as "meditation" (*sgom*) is used to describe both even though they are distinctly different, one referring to the cultivation of subjective awareness and the other to the cultivation of objective clarity.

Just as muddy water is not very good for showing reflections, the mind muddied by laxity and lethargy is not suitable for reflection of the clarity of the object of meditation. Thus laxity and lethargy are obstacles for gaining higher realizations.

Like laxity, excitement draws the mind away from the object of meditation. At that point, however, their similarities end, because excitement distracts the mind, focusing in an outward direction toward an object of attachment or aversion. It leads the mind into a state of forgetfulness, more specifically, forgetfulness of the object of meditation. In this forgetful condition, although the mind is excited and distracted, its clarity is intact and strong, albeit extremely unstable.

Indeed, two qualities of mind are necessary if one is to overcome the obstacles to the attainment of higher realization. One is strength of clarity; the other is non-discursive stability.

Imagine being utterly enthralled and engrossed in something that is enormously attractive. You are so captivated by it, so held in its sway that you forget everything else. Imagine listening to a piece of enchanting music. Imagine the mind becoming so completely drawn into it, so captivated by it, that you are hardly aware of what appears in your field of vision. That is stability.

When stability* arises in your meditation, even though you have the sense of having been sitting for only a short while, when you come out of it you find that much more time has passed than you had expected. On the other hand, when stability is lacking you will find yourself looking at your wristwatch an awful lot.

To cultivate śamatha, we need both strength of clarity as well as non-discursive stability. If one is endowed with both, it is said that one is a very suitable vessel for the cultivation of the path. Generally speaking, the concentration which leads to the path and propels one along the path is a state of mind which is single-pointedly focused upon its object. For the cultivation of proper concentration there are two essential ingredients: One of these is mindfulness—the ability to maintain continuity of awareness of the object. The second is vigilance—the mental faculty of guarding or watching over the meditative process to recognize if distraction has occurred. These must be cultivated in the course of the practice.

## MAINTAINING AWARENESS OF THE OBJECT

Let us examine the object of the breath in terms of cultivating śamatha. How does one maintain mindfulness of the breathing process? By focusing the mind upon it with continuity. It is said that there is no other cultivation of concentration* apart from the very process of cultivating or maintaining mindfulness. That is, if you are cultivating mindfulness of the breath, that itself is the very means of developing concentration. You do not have to add anything else to the process.

There are different techniques of breath awareness. For example, you can follow the path of the breath through the nasal passages, into the lungs, and back up through the nasal passages. You can concentrate on the rise and fall of the abdomen, or simply be focused on the tactile sensations in a specific point at the tip of the nose as the breath passes in and out of the body.

If the object of meditation is the image of the Buddha, initially one directs the mind to the object, scrutinizing it part by part—where the hands are placed, the position of the head, legs, torso, etc. Having done that, simply apprehend the object in its entirety and maintain that awareness. Do not engage in any kind of analysis or checking up of the object. One simply remains with it and cultivates stability. This is exactly what is referred to as non-discursive stability.

Once you have arrived at this point in meditation, if a particular part of the Buddha image becomes very clear, simply focus on that part because of its special clarity. Then, gradually, gradually clarity will spread to the rest of the object. This does not mean that you focus on that part to the exclusion of the rest of the image. What it does mean is that you give greater emphasis to that area of clarity while maintaining a general awareness of the entire object of visualization. So, on the one hand you have general awareness of the whole image, and on the other you place greater emphasis on any part that may be appearing more vividly.

Aśvagoṣa, the great Indian pandit and contemplative, said that if one maintains awareness of one object, this will give rise to a stability in one's awareness; whereas if one shifts around, jumps from one object to another, this will prevent the arising of stability and fatigue the mind.

If your object is the breath, whatever technique you choose to follow, maintain just that until you move on to the next stage of the practice. If you are following the movement of the abdomen, maintain continuity, stay with it. Do not move on to concentrating on the tactile sensation at the tip of the nose.

Similarly, if you are focusing on the Buddha image, do not allow that image to change, even though it may begin to do so by itself. For example, in the case that you have chosen an image of the Buddha sitting in full lotus, if the image stands up, tell it to sit right back down. If it suddenly changes its color to yellow or red, make it go back to what it was. Maintain your root object and do not allow it to change.

## ANTIDOTES TO LAXITY AND EXCITEMENT

Mindfulness and vigilance are the antidotes, or remedial applications, to laxity and excitement. As the practice proceeds, one's chief concern should be with mindfulness, focusing on the object of meditation. However, one part of one's awareness should be devoted to vigilance.

If you err in this technique, giving too much emphasis to vigilance, what should be an antidote will become an obstruction, and mindfulness will deteriorate. In this case, your whole practice will deteriorate. The reason for this is that the two objects apprehended by these two faculties are different. Mindfulness is focused on the chief object, be it the breath or the Buddha image. In contrast, vigilance is focused on the meditation itself, the quality of the meditative awareness. It is intermittently checking up to see whether that meditative awareness is too tight or too loose. If mindfulness is concentrated at the tip of your nose, then properly directed and balanced vigilance attends to the awareness itself. If too much energy goes into vigilance, awareness of the breath deteriorates. This is one of the most fundamental points to be kept in mind throughout the meditation.

In terms of the strength of clarity, as well as the manner in which the mind apprehends its object, each person needs to find the appropriate degree of tension that is neither too tight nor too loose. If the strength of clarity is too high, this agitates the mind. If it is too low, then lethargy or laxity arises. There is no set formula to the equation. It is something one has to determine for oneself, finding that middle ground, walking the razor's edge between agitation and laxity. It is indeed in the middle way that you must cultivate stability.

Vigilance is a mental factor that must be totally adaptable to the needs of the moment. It has different functions on different occasions.

When the mind is stable, it is not subject to scattering* and excitement.* It is, however, prone to the dangers of laxity. Thus, when the mind is stable, the special task of vigilance is to guard against laxity, and it must wield a double-edged sword. On the one hand, it must be watchful to see if laxity is arising. On the other, it is concerned with the strength of clarity, the direct antidote to laxity.

When strength of clarity is present, then it is the special task of vigilance to be on guard against the arising of scattering and excitement. It must be watchful to see that the desired strength of clarity is balanced by stability. Working at its fullest efficiency, vigilance checks the level of tension in the mind. When the mind is getting a bit tense, lighten up a little. If it is getting too slack, tighten up a bit.

Vigilance is a mental factor, but if one looks for it in the Buddhist psychological presentation of the fifty-one mental factors* it is not to be found. Why is that? Because it is included in the mental factor of intelligence.*

Within the parameters of intelligence, there is both a distorted intelligence as well as a non-distorted intelligence. Vigilance is, by definition, only the non-distorted form.

Even though vigilance is not included in the fifty-one mental factors, non-vigilance is included as one of the twenty secondary mental distortions. What is the nature of non-vigilance? It is a mental factor having the function of not discerning activities of the three doors of body, speech and mind.

This means that non-vigilance is not aware of the quality of that behavior that is being impelled by attachment, anger, and other various afflictions. In that this is the very definition of non-vigilance, we can see that vigilance implicitly also entails discernment with regards to the wholesome and unwholesome. The function of non-vigilance is to distract one from wholesome activity, whereas vigilance entails not being distracted from the wholesome.

## DISPELLING A FAULTY APPROACH

If you do not concern yourself with the strength of clarity, you will find that stability is more easily maintained. There is a well-known Buddhist aphorism that can easily be misinterpreted: "The best relaxation is the best meditation." If you take that literally, you can ascend to the heights of laxity and confuse that state of laxity—which does have stability—for proper meditation. This would be a faulty approach.

Because an essential attribute of laxity is lack of clarity, it does not provide the basis for gaining higher and higher realizations. The quality of mind upon full awakening is one of extraordinary lucidity and clarity—that is the end product. If you are cultivating laxity, your clarity will be on a downward path, which clearly indicates that you are not going toward full awakening. Simply and directly, the way to dispel a faulty approach is to be on guard for laxity and to apply antidotes the moment you see it arise.

## DURATION OF SESSIONS

It is said that at the outset of the practice, because one is still very prone to excitement and scattering, one should keep the sessions short and have many of them. One suggestion is that each session be one *chu-tsö*, which is twenty-four minutes (i.e., one-sixtieth of a night and day). This is only a suggestion, not a strong rule. You might begin with just fifteen-minute sessions. Within that period, check up closely to see how strongly excitement and scattering are affecting your mind. If you are falling prey to either, diminish the length of the session.

It is said that when you find and focus on your object the mind has a certain power to it. If you totally lose the object, when your mind refocuses it has somewhat less power. If you lose the object twice, the mind has still less power. If you lose it a third time, it is said that you might as well give up, end that session, wait a while and start again. Here is the situation: You are sitting in meditation and you hear some abrupt sound. It punches a hole in your awareness and you lose the object. A second sound punches two holes. A third sound punches another hole and your awareness is leaking all over the place. Now it is better to stop and pick it up again when you can bring back the full strength of your meditation.

The point here is to cultivate a high quality of awareness, to try to extend the duration of that high quality, and to avoid sitting around with a muddled awareness for a very long time. When you begin, of course, you will find that there is a tendency to fall prey frequently to both excitement and laxity. If you sit in meditation and continuously succumb to these faults, you are not cultivating a faultless approach to concentration.

## UNDERSTANDING THAT ARISES FROM REFLECTION

All of the teachings here are important. There is nothing superfluous. Yet, these particular points are especially important because they concern the very techniques you will be using day to day, sitting to sitting, moment to moment. It is essential that you become very familiar with them, really absorb them, integrate them into your practice, make them your own. It will take a little time, but gradually, by the very process of meditation, you will begin to realize the significance of each point. That realization is the key to progress. It is not sufficient to think that you have an intellectual understanding. To think, "I've got it!" is not enough, because as long as you are still thinking, *you do not have it.*

There are different levels of understanding. The first is one that arises from hearing. This is where you are right now, hearing sounds, hearing words, hearing concepts. But hearing is not the same as deeper understanding, and it is only when you actually start implementing this advice in your practice that through your own experience you will start that process of realization. Only then will you start recognizing, "Oh, this is what that meant!" At that point, there arises a deeper level of understanding known as "understanding that arises from reflection."

## QUESTIONS AND ANSWERS

**Q:** How can one develop greater clarity without yielding to scattering, tensing up the mind, and giving rise to stress?

**A:** As one is cultivating stability, one should be especially on guard for the arising of laxity. For the development of clarity, the mind needs to be elated, aroused. This can be done by means of reflecting on uplifting subjects, the fully endowed human life, the benefits of śamatha, and the like. As you set forth in the meditation, you must alternate the emphases in the practice: being on guard for the arising of laxity and watching carefully the state of your clarity; and being on guard against excitement or scattering and checking on the strength of your stability.

So, at first you are emphasizing one, then the other, and no one but you can determine what the suitable level of awareness is. When you are developing the strength of clarity, there is a tendency for excitement to arise. If you feel it arising, taper off a bit on the clarity side. Likewise, when you are going for stability, you are prone to laxity arising. When you see that happening, then you want to uplift the mind. What you want is to balance right in the middle. The middle is something that can only be sought out by means of your own experience.

Essentially, we find ourselves in the predicament of Candragomin, who wrote a verse that can be paraphrased: "When I increase my enthusiasm, going for clarity, my mind gets excited; whereas when my mind gets more stable I tend more towards laxity. I find it very hard to find that middle ground. What am I to do?"

What you do is gradually seek out that middle path by means of your own experience. The more you practice, the more experience you acquire, and the more clarity you gain as to how to develop your practice.

One thing to remember as you enter the first stages of practice is that at the outset there tends to be a strong urge to get better clarity fast. Don't go for it. Be satisfied with a rather poor quality of clarity and really go for stability. The appropriate process is to start by trying to establish stability in a very gradual and gentle way. Upon that basis, clarity can then be developed. In the early stages of your practice it may be that clarity is surprisingly good. Because the mind is so prone to attachment and excitement you may feel the irresistible urge to go for even more clarity. It's a trap. If you follow that route the clarity will become an obstacle. Therefore, first of all, emphasize stability.

**Q:** If the object is very clearly appearing, doesn't this imply that there is already strength of clarity in terms of your mode of apprehending the object?

**A:** No. In this case, it is said that when subtle laxity* occurs, there is clarity of the object, not as clear as you would see it with your eyes, but still quite clear. It is because there isn't the strength of clarity in the mode of apprehension that subtle laxity is present. Don't be complacent too soon. Even though it seems quite clear, you must make sure that subjective rather than objective clarity is the cause of its vividness.

**Q:** What about the duration of a session? Must it be only fifteen minutes, or can it be longer?

**A:** However long it may be, what is most important during the course of each meditation session is that you not fall prey to either laxity or excitement. So, if a half hour has gone by and you are really aiming at fifteen minutes, this is suggestive of reasonably good quality. The time passed and you were not aware of it.

The crucial thing is not how many minutes passed, but that you do not indulge in a meditation after being heavily subject to excitement and laxity. If you find that you are thinking fifteen minutes have gone by but in actuality it has been an hour, it can start to be a habit that you overshoot the time mark. In the beginning, it is preferable to keep the session at fifteen minutes and shoot for the highest quality of awareness during that time. It is said that if you develop a strong resolve to stop at fifteen minutes, even in the midst of stability you will have a subconscious alarm clock that will just go off and bring you out of it.

There is a story of two men on their way from Kham to Lhasa. One was a strong meditator. Every morning he would meditate while the other cooked breakfast. When his companion called out, "Tea is on!" the meditator would break off his session. This went on until the companion grew tired of the meditator's "laziness." One day, instead of saying, "Tea is on!" he ate his own breakfast, left the meditator on the trail, and continued the journey all by himself. Arriving in Lhasa after several days, he went to see Pha-bong-kha, who inquired about the meditator's whereabouts. Learning that he was still sitting out there on the trail, Pha-bong-kha told the traveler to return immediately and arouse the meditator from his state of concentration.

The man retraced his steps back up the trail and found the meditator still sitting in concentration, just as he had left him days before. At that point, he made breakfast and called out, "Tea is on!" Hearing him, the meditator arose, ate his breakfast, and the two of them went on to Lhasa.

The meditator had great stability but not much discipline. In a very specific way he was lazy, just as his companion thought he was. The truth of the matter is that the force of anticipation, determination and resolve are very effective, and you can pretty much determine the length of your own sessions even without an alarm clock. This is true in sleep as well as in meditation. If you really set the resolve, you probably can do it.

**Q:** Could you elaborate a little bit about distractions "punching holes in your meditation"? You hear a sound and that takes your mind away from the object. If a thought comes up, that too takes your mind away from the object. Are you saying that we should end a session any time our mind conceptualizes more than three thoughts?

**A:** That statement about losing it three times really refers to the case when you have quite good stability, when you really are an experienced meditator. In that case, if a loud sound or anything else of the kind comes a third time, stop your session.

At the beginning the stability is not that great. In that case, rather than counting off, "one, two, three," and then cutting your meditation short, check the state of your awareness. If it isn't that bad after three thoughts or sounds, carry on. But if you find that it is getting very muggy, whether it is after two minutes or twenty minutes, stop. Once you have lost the power of the mind, then there is no point in being insistent and grinding away.

Don't be too rigid about the duration of your sessions. If the quality of the mind has diminished before fifteen minutes have gone by, then bring the session to a close after just seven or eight minutes. On the other hand, if the power of the mind is good and strong at the end of a fifteen-minute session, and you are not really very subject to distraction or laxity, there is no problem in letting it go on a little longer.

There is a point when you will extend the designated duration of your sessions, but you don't want to be too hasty about doing that. For example, if you have a morning session in which the quality of the mind is quite good and you let that particular session go on a little bit longer, that is no problem. But that does not necessarily mean that your other sessions in the afternoon or evening are going to be that good. You must not think, "I've done so well that I can go longer on all of them" or, "Since yesterday was so good, it will be that good today and tomorrow." The time to begin thinking about extending the general length of the session to twenty minutes, or whatever limit you have in mind, is when you find that stability is really good session after session. Be in tune with the quality of the mind from session to session, whether you had to end this one at seven minutes, or let the last one go to twenty minutes. Be flexible. Session by session, let the length be governed by the quality of your awareness.

**Q:** Sometimes I am clear about whether or not I'm losing the object. If I go daydreaming, I know I've lost the object. But there are others times, for instance, when I hear a bell or thoughts come to my mind, and it seems like I am still on the object. I'm aware that a lot of things are going on and I don't know if I am holding two objects at one time or not.

**A:** This is a very important point that we will be discussing fully a little later, so right now I'll just give a brief answer. First of all, if you are focusing on the object and you hear a sound or a thought arises, and you feel that you are doing two things at once, you can be sure that you are.

This is where you must learn to distinguish between gross excitement* and subtle excitement.* When you are daydreaming, that is gross excitement, the mind has left its object completely and gone elsewhere. In the case of subtle excitement, the mind can be wandering around and at the same time still be focused on the object. It is doing both.

Both excitement and laxity are considered to be forms of distraction. With laxity the mind is distracted inwards, whereas with excitement the mind is distracted outwards. Other important terms: scattering and lethargy.

When you reach the fourth mental state* you won't lose your object completely again. That is because in the fourth mental state one has abandoned gross excitement, which means that in your meditation you are no longer subject to losing your object. But subtle excitement (when you are focusing on the object and yet the mind is a bit distracted) is not abandoned until the eighth mental state. And that is way up there!

**Q:** Does that mean you won't lose the object within a specific session, or is that just a stage of practice that continues from day to day?

**A:** Once one has firmly attained the fourth mental state, this entails the abandonment of gross excitement. From that point forward, whenever you are practicing śamatha, you are not prone to losing the object completely. You still have to be watchful, however. It is possible that you could lose the object if your metabolism is disturbed in some way, by eating bad food or getting too physically active. You are not so free that you can put your feet up and say, "I don't have to be concerned with it any more." You still have to be aware, but it isn't a real problem any longer.

**Q:** In my case, the object is growing bigger. I know it isn't supposed to do that, but there seems to be tremendous tension involved in trying to squeeze it back to size. Is it better at that point to end the session, or to persist in trying to reduce it?

**A:** For the time being, simply start the session, but start it with a certain awareness of that issue. Be clearly aware that it is your mind that is making the object bigger. It is not anything from the side of the object. The *image* is not doing it, *you* are doing it. Try to meditate in such a way that you have the proper image and bring the session to a close when the image begins to grow in size. It's no big problem if some of your sessions are only three or four minutes long. Most important is quality.

**Q:** Should we be visualizing the Buddha image at the level of the navel, at the heart or on the top of the head?

**A:** According to tradition, if one visualizes the object higher one will thereby be prone to the arising of tension as well as excitement. For that reason it is generally suggested that you visualize it lower.

To prevent it from rising, or growing, for a couple of days visualize the Buddha image as being very heavy. Another possibility for keeping the energies down is to imagine yourself with a heavy double-crossed vajra on the top of your head. That can be done when you are subject to strong excitement, or when energy is starting to rise. Don't do it when you are subject to laxity.

**Q:** How should we go about deciding which object to focus on, the Buddha image or the breath? Shall we try them both and see how they are? Should we spend all of a day on one and then try a day with the other?

**A:** Check it out. You can try it that way, or maybe do a morning on one and an afternoon on the other. It's not a big deal.

If, in the course of your practice, you decide to focus on the Buddha image, it is certainly more difficult. However, if you feel that you have some chance there, it would not be a bad choice. By the time you get to the fifth, sixth, seventh and eighth states, then it is really easy to create it and visualize it.

**Q:** If we have thoughts and feelings that act as interruptions, what is the correct attitude towards them during the session?

**A:** Such things are included in two categories with which we are already familiar: scattering and excitement. This being the case, having recognized that certain thoughts or emotions have arisen, simply release them and come back to the object. If you find that the straightforward process does not work, then go on to one of the reflections to sober the mind, e.g., meditation on the suffering of saṃsāra, impermanence, and other subjects.

As an antidote for both excitement and scattering, the mind needs to be de-pressed a little bit, it needs to be pressed *down*. When the mind is too far down, or drawn inward, in terms of laxity, it needs to be uplifted.

At times when feelings become a distraction, meditate on impermanence. Be they happy and pleasurable feelings, or unhappy and painful feelings, recognize that they come in dependence upon a collection of causes and conditions, and pass in dependence upon a collection of causes and conditions. When that is deeply understood, there is no reason to become involved in them.

**Q:** There are two different techniques of visualizing the Buddha image—one is in the space before you and the other is the self-generation as the Buddha. The question is whether "divine pride" applies to both or just to the latter case?

**A:** It applies only in self-generation. If you are doing self-generation, first of all, you are Dorje Chang (Buddha Vajradhara). Then you transform that into the Buddha Śakyamuni. This is in the case of integrating Six-Session Guru Yoga and śamatha, where you start off by visualizing yourself as Vajradhara.

If you are not integrating the Six-Session Guru Yoga into the practice, but are simply visualizing the Buddha in the space before you, divine pride does not apply.

# 8 Meditating on Impermanence

It is stated in the *sūtras** that whatever arises must inevitably be destroyed, that each phenomenon has the quality of passing away. This tells us that from the very moment of its arising, every phenomenon that is created has the nature of dissolution. In this context, the meaning of the term *momentary impermanence* is that phenomena do not even abide in sameness for one single moment.

Meditating on impermanence, one can identify two points in the existence of any phenomenon: the point in time of its creation, and the point in time of its destruction. Prior to the production of this world, for example, there was only empty space. The world was created, and following the dissolution or passing away of this world, there will remain only empty space.

Similarly, any interval of time, whether it is a cosmic cycle or simply an hour, has its parameters—its beginning and its end. We see that it passes minute by minute, yet another interval of time. The minute has its parameters as well. We can see that it passes through each second. Going deeper, it is possible to take a second and divide it up into moments, and portions of moments, each one having its point of arising and its point of passing away. As we make a closer and more profound inspection in meditation, it becomes apparent that none of these segments of time has any absolute, inherent duration at all.

Returning our attention to this world, we recognize that from the time of its creation to the time of its dissolution it does not abide in sameness for even a minute, even though that is not immediately recognizable in the way the world appears to us. All the things around us appear to be relatively static in spite of the fact that they actually exist in this utterly momentary fashion, without abiding. Just as we can take a minute and see how it is changing second by second, so we can take this whole world and see that each of its moments is in the process of change, in the process of changing in the direction of its own dissolution or vanishing.

We tend to be attached to our own bodies, to see them as permanent, but this body too has its parameters. It too is in a constant state of change, and the direction in which it moves with each moment of change is towards its own destruction. Everything around us, our parents, our children, our friends, all material things to which we are attached—each of these is in a continual state of change and moving toward its own dissolution.

As we look at the various types of mental distortions—be it attachment, anger, jealousy, competitiveness, to name a few— we can see that each of these afflictions is based on the assumption of some kind of remaining substance, on our immortality or theirs. Grasping onto these things and events as somehow being of an unchanging nature stimulates an emotional response: "Oh, I did not get this," or "I was disappointed here," or "My desires were not satisfied there." All these responses are based on the illusory sense that things need not change and are not in a constant state of change. These are the very same mental distortions that lead us to desire things "out there," and through the frustration of these desires we encounter the suffering that comes to the body as well as the mind. It is well worth the time to contemplate this subject: that all suffering arises in dependence upon a confused state of mind.

If we can really become familiar with the inevitability of constant change and impermanence—when we are at times compelled to part from friends, parents, loved ones, from all the things to which we are attached—in each of these cases we can respond with aplomb, simply recognizing that all these phenomena are of the nature of things from which one must be separated. With this insight, attachment does not arise, we are not disturbed, and we are not subject to the anxiety that would otherwise arise in the face of parting with such things. This relates directly to Śantideva's statement which can be paraphrased as: When one being is an utterly changing phenomenon, not remaining even for a moment but in a constant state of change, and another being is also in a constant state of change, how can there be attachment by one for the other? He is telling us that in that situation, attachment is a very inappropriate response.

If we have contemplated upon this sufficiently, when suffering arises from attachment we can go back to Śantideva's wisdom: When I am totally impermanent and the other is totally impermanent, how can there be attachment by one for the other? This is not an antidote for attachment alone. It works equally well with anger: When I am impermanent and the other is impermanent, how can there be anger of one for the other? It works in the same way with competitiveness, jealousy, arrogance or pride. In each of these situations the same verse can be a powerful aid for changing and relaxing the mind. The situation that frustrates you, that disappoints you, is the result of causes and conditions. The causes and conditions will change, and the situation will pass. This is how the mind finds calm and equanimity.

During meditation, in the face of excitement arising from attachment, or when you feel exalted or excited about something, bring out the same thought: This situation that excites me is something arising in dependence upon causes and conditions. It has the nature to pass away and I shall be separated from it.

It is said that of all the recognitions and discernments, the greatest is the discernment of impermanence. The first of the Four Noble Truths is the truth of suffering. When the nature of suffering is investigated in detail, the truth of impermanence inevitably appears. The realization of impermanence leads to the realization of suffering, and this, in turn, can lead to a realization of selflessness. In a narrower sense, the same recognition of impermanence can be applied as an antidote to both excitement and laxity.

# 9 How One Performs After Directing the Mind to the Object

## THE PRACTICE WHEN EITHER LAXITY OR EXCITEMENT ARISES

*The Definition of Laxity*

Laxity is defined as a mental factor which is distracted inwardly, while cultivating virtue, due to a diminishing of the strength of clarity. Its direct function is to obstruct clarity. Its indirect function is to obstruct the attainment of meditative quiescence.

While it is a mental factor, it is not to be found among the fifty-one mental factors. However, you can find it implicitly either under lethargy, which is included, or under distraction, which is also included. Although you could subsume laxity under either lethargy or distraction, it is not either as they are defined. The reason for this is that both distraction and lethargy are unwholesome mental factors, whereas laxity, at least in one sense, may be wholesome in that the mental state during laxity may be benevolent. Thus it is possible to have a wholesome mind that is, nevertheless, at the same time subject to laxity. For that reason, it cannot be included under the umbrella of either lethargy or distraction.

The aspect of laxity is either some mental darkness, a little bit of gloominess—gloominess in the cognitive rather than the emotional sense—or simply one of being too relaxed. Having lost its grip, it reacts inwardly.

Gross laxity* is a form of laxity, so it fits the preceding definition. However, gross laxity entails a lack of lucidity and lack of strength of clarity, both of these from the subject's side. In other words, the subject, the mind itself, lacks the strength of clarity and lucidity, so that the forceful apprehension of the object has been lost or has largely slacked off.

Subtle laxity is a form of laxity in which you have some lucidity and some strength of clarity—not that there is a big difference between the two—but the force of apprehension of the object is slightly slacked off.

Gross and subtle laxity are spoken of as if there were only two degrees, but one finds in practice that there are many gradations that range from extremely gross—the first type experienced—and extremely subtle laxity, until the seventh mental state, in which you are still subject to the most subtle form of laxity. Complete freedom from laxity is reached in the eighth mental state.

Lethargy is similar to laxity, but it is not the same. Lethargy is a mental factor included within one of the six primary mental distortions, the mental distortion variously called delusion, confusion, or bewilderment. Its function is that it obstructs the attainment of śamatha.

Lethargy and laxity are companions. Laxity leads, lethargy follows, and they both run in the same direction. After a heavy meal we often experience a sense of heaviness of body and mind. We want to lie back and get into a horizontal position. Even the face can feel heavy. The mind feels sluggish. All of these are aspects of lethargy.

In meditation, the sequence of arising of these various mental factors has a definite pattern: Imagine starting with a good strength of clarity of mind, which degenerates to the point where laxity arises; laxity follows its course, giving

rise to lethargy; lethargy follows its course, leading into
sleep. It is a natural progression.

### The Definition of Excitement

Excitement is a state of mind that occurs when focusing upon
a sensual object with which one is previously acquainted, and
it causes the mind to be scattered outwards. The mental factor of excitement apprehends the object in the mode of craving. Its function is to obstruct śamatha.

Gross excitement arises when the mind does not remain on
the object despite the fact that one has applied the antidotes
to excitement.

In the case of subtle excitement the mind is not scattered
away from the object, although the awareness does not remain
entirely on the object. The awareness is divided.

Just as in the case of laxity, you cannot speak of excitement
as having only two degrees. Experientially one finds that there
are many gradations between very gross and very subtle excitement, right up to the seventh mental state. At this point
there remains only the most subtle excitement, and that is abandoned upon the attainment of the eighth mental state.

Scattering is a mental factor that is similar to excitement.
Yet there are distinctions between the two. Excitement, by its
very definition, is something that draws attention away from
the object of meditation by the force of attachment, craving
and lust. Scattering also draws the attention away from the
object, but it is not necessarily propelled by attachment. It
may be propelled by some virtuous topic or may be conjoined
with some other mental distortion apart from attachment.

Among the twenty secondary mental distortions, remove excitement and you are left with nineteen, all of which are various forms of scattering: scattering conjoined with pride, with
anger, jealousy, laziness, and many others. In addition, if
thoughts of bodhicitta, meditation on emptiness, thoughts of
developing renunciation, or an emergent mind arise during
the cultivation of śamatha, all of those, too, would be forms
of scattering.

## CULTIVATING VIGILANCE THAT RECOGNIZES LAXITY AND EXCITEMENT

It is essential to have an understanding of the definitions of laxity and excitement, and yet mere intellectual understanding is not enough. In addition one needs to ascertain each mental factor as it arises during meditation. Even beyond that, it is important to acquire the more subtle capacity to recognize laxity and excitement when they are on the verge of arising.

It is through the gradual cultivation of vigilance that one is able to recognize laxity and excitement, first as they arise, and second when they are on the verge of arising. As the practice progresses, vigilance increases in its effectiveness until, upon the attainment of the sixth mental state, one's powers of vigilance are strong enough occasionally to recognize both mental factors on the verge of their arising. In the seventh mental state, one knows they are on the way well before they arise. It's a little like waiting for a train and knowing it is about to pull into the station before you can see it on the track. Not only can you hear it, you can also see the conductors, the porters, and the engineers move into action.

The power of mindfulness is developed in the third and fourth mental states, and attained upon the completion of the fourth. It is during the fifth and sixth mental states that the power of vigilance is developed, and it is upon the attainment of the sixth that it is perfected.

In terms of the practice, it is essential to maintain mindfulness—firmly holding onto the object—at all times. The logical question is, Is vigilance something that you also maintain constantly? The answer is an emphatic *no!*

It is said that vigilance is something that is to be applied only intermittently. Especially at the beginning stages, you need to be very aware of how frequently and when to intrude in the meditation, watching and checking up with vigilance. You must quickly become sensitive to the general condition of the mind. When it is pretty well free of laxity and excitement, leave it alone. When it is more likely to be prone to the laxity and excitement, that is the time to bring in your guardian, vigilance.

Vigilance can arise casually or intuitively as well. If the force of one's mindfulness is quite strong, vigilance easily arises on its own. Similarly, if vigilance is strong, it is easy for mindfulness to be maintained. In the *Guide to the Bodhisattva's Way of Life*, Śantideva says that if mindfulness is strong, even when it is not manifesting, vigilance will be nearby and will easily manifest.

If one places a high value on the Buddha's teachings and on the instructions of one's spiritual mentor, and if one has a fear of rebirth in lower realms and also an appreciation of the excellent qualities of bodhicitta, the path of awakening and full buddhahood, then mindfulness is easily generated. Laxity and excitement are listed jointly as the third of the five faults that act as obstructions to śamatha. The antidote for this fault is vigilance. Therefore, it is said that upon the recognition of either laxity or excitement, one should generate vigilance and apply other more indirect antidotes which will be discussed a little later.

## THE FOURTH FAULT: NON-APPLICATION

Non-application* is the failure to apply the antidotes when laxity or excitement arise. In this case, the problem has arisen, you have recognized that the problem has arisen, and you respond with non-application, that is, you do not respond at all. This is a fault.

## THE ANTIDOTE TO NON-APPLICATION

Very simply, the antidote to non-application is application,* or just *doing something about it.*

What is the nature of application?

When one has recognized the arising of either laxity or excitement, but does nothing, the function of application is to move the awareness right back to the object, where it can pick up the continuity of mindfulness. The intention to redirect the awareness is the immediate, first-stage remedy. Essentially, it says "Come back!" If the mind obeys, it is back on track. If the mind does not come back to the object, then additional antidotes have to be applied.

### The Definition of Intention

Intention* is a mental factor having the function of directing the mind and the mental factors with which it is conjoined towards a given object. It is the "mover of the mind." Intention directs not only the principal consciousness itself, but all of the concomitant, or simultaneously arising, factors of the mind. They all occupy the same vehicle and go in the same direction, and the driver is intention.

When with vigilance one suspects the presence of laxity, one must clearly distinguish between the objective and subjective strength of clarity. Refer back to the original discussion of this subject and remember that clarity of the object is not something that is likely to occur at the beginning of the practice. It will come about very gradually. However, the subjective strength of clarity of awareness is something that must be present right from the beginning. If one fails to make that distinction, it will be hard, if not impossible, to develop stability.

This point cannot be emphasized too strongly. First concentrate on stability. When stability is fairly good—not *very* good, just pretty good—then slowly shift the emphasis to the strength of clarity of the apprehending mind. If you have no stability and try to make the shift with nothing but sheer determination—because that's what it boils down to—you will destroy the possibility of getting any stability at all. Please hold this very, very firmly in your mind. Don't lose it. And when you sit down to meditate, apply it!

## ADDITIONAL REMEDIES FOR LAXITY

When the mind has wandered off due to laxity, and intention does not bring it back to the object of meditation, you must temporarily set the object aside and do something else. You might begin by visualizing your body filled with light.

Another way to counteract laxity is to broaden your mind, cheer it up, give it more space, uplift the spirit. It is important to apply this technique by focusing upon wholesome objects, not something that merely stimulates your mental distortions. Wholesome objects could be the excellent qualities of fully awakened beings, demonstrations of kindness of the fully awakened beings, the benefits of bodhicitta, the value and rarity of a fully endowed human life, or the qualities of one's spiritual mentor.

It is better not to interrupt the meditation for an extensive analytical meditation. In order to avoid that necessity, it is helpful to have a little nugget of something to think about, not very elaborate, but something that takes the essence of the subject. Use this to uplift your mind. If you have difficulty finding the right nugget, consult your mentor and ask him to help you come up with something concise.

It is my impression that Westerners are not too interested in meditating on suffering. On first impression it is a practice that seems depressing. The trouble is that when one does not meditate on suffering but looks only for happy things to think about, later, when it comes time to contemplate the kindness of the Buddha or the benefits of bodhicitta, these topics do not have much power. As one meditates on the excellent qualities of the Buddha, the Dharma and the Saṅgha, one finds joy in them because they are so effective in eradicating suffering. If suffering is not an issue, they are just a waste of time.

In using this meditative remedy, don't expect immediate results. They may appear, but don't expect them. Nevertheless, when you are confronted by the repeated arising of laxity, continue to meditate on uplifting subjects. You may not feel the effect in the next meditation, but very likely the next day you will feel it.

Other remedies to laxity relate more to physical conditions. Stay cool. If you find heat is making you sluggish, you might want to wear lighter clothes or increase the ventilation in your room. Another remedy is diet. Some people find that the mind goes lax when they are eating rich foods, but it can also happen when your food is not nutritious enough. Extremes either way can cause laxity. You must check it out for yourselves. Be mindful of what you eat and watch how it affects your meditations.

It is also said that it can be of benefit to gaze out over a distant horizon, something far away. Look at the sky. Look at light, anything that is bright. Make sure that your room is bright, that you do not sit in gloom. Be certain to shower often enough. If you do not bathe frequently enough it can give rise to laxity, not to mention complaints from your fellow meditators. There are limits, of course. If you find yourself getting drowsy, you shouldn't spend all your time in the shower.

There are gentle and forceful means for dispelling laxity. One forceful means is to follow the practical guidance from Pa-dam-pa Sang-gye. You visualize your mind as a little sphere of radiant white light at your heart. Then, with a forceful exhalation from the diaphragm, very vigorously send it right up through the central channel and out through the crown of your head. As you do this, say the word *Phat!* Of course, if you are meditating within earshot of other people, either say "Phat!" silently to yourself or just imagine the light going up into space and merging with it.

Another visualization that can dispel laxity is to imagine yourself sitting on top of a telephone pole. That should wake anybody up. But if even that doesn't work, then imagine yourself sitting on top of a telephone pole during an earthquake.

## ADDITIONAL REMEDIES FOR EXCITEMENT

Just as is the case with laxity, when intention does not subdue excitement, additional remedial measures require you to leave the major object of meditation. Here too, meditative or reflective remedies can be effective. As it has been stated in *The Essence of the Middle Way* by Bhāvaviveka, the mind can be pacified or calmed in the face of excitement by directing the attention to topics such as the suffering nature of the cycle of existence, the suffering nature of the lower realms of existence, impermanence, or compassion. The purpose of all these reflective meditations is to sober the mind, to bring it down.

Many events and circumstances of worldly life attract our attention. Just by watching television we can see accounts of the slaughter of animals and fish, the savagery and killing that goes on in the animal kingdom, animals fighting each other and eating each other, and the human mistreatment of animals. The TV is a window to the extent of human suffering as well. Without even going into the street to see homeless and hungry people begging in doorways, the evening news forces us to witness the tremendous hardships and travails of famine, of war, revolts, revolutions, demonstrations, imprisonment, torture, brutality. The contemplation of these aspects of suffering combined with the cultivation of compassion for the beings experiencing that suffering will sober the mind and allow awareness to be drawn in once again.

There are many different ways of meditating on impermanence that will also draw the mind inward. One of the foremost is the meditation on death—of close friends and family, and your own death—as one manifestation of impermanence. Another is the four-fold theme:

> All acquisition ends in dispersion,
> All building ends in destruction,
> All meetings end in parting,
> All births end in death.

Let us examine just one of these four themes—"All meetings end in parting." Take this meeting as an example, or a gathering of a few friends. The usual response to this kind of event is one of delight, the happiness of being together; but usually that delight is tainted with attachment. If, on the other hand, we look at this same event with wisdom and intelligence, we will recognize that in the simple event of gathering, the cause for parting is simultaneously born. Separation does not have to wait for another cause to arise. The cause is already there and parting is inevitable. This being the case, if we look at the gathering in its fullness, we realize that it is not a cause for rejoicing, attachment or excitement; neither is it a cause for remorse or unhappiness. We simply see it as it is, in its entirety.

Armed with that insight of wisdom, one realizes that "All births end in death." There is absolutely no question that all of the participants of the gathering are going to die. This obviously includes the inevitability that they are going to be separated. That does not require any further logical analysis. This clear insight will act as an antidote for the attachment-delight arising from gathering, as well as the aversion-unhappiness that comes in the face of parting. The antidote to attachment and aversion is to see the whole picture with clarity and wisdom.

Another antidote to attachment is simply to focus on change—not impermanence, just gross change. See the various events of this world and recognize that they have arisen from causes that are at this very moment in the process of change, and moreover that the process of change must and will continue. As it is for the things around us, so it is for the planet as a whole. It, too, arose and is in a continual process of change. Focusing on that change dissolves attachment which derives from viewing phenomena in their static or immutable aspect.

In *A Guide to the Bodhisattva's Way of Life*, Śāntideva states that every person is an ever-changing sequence of events, that other people are ever-changing series of events. Then he asks: How can one phenomenon that is in a continual state of change be attached to another phenomenon that is also in a continual state of change? That and many other antidotes to attachment can be found in the eighth chapter of that text. The first chapter discusses the benefits of bodhicitta quite elaborately. The latter part of the third chapter goes into the many ways to view impermanence. It is a good guidebook for meditative remedies to laxity and excitement.

If you find that the reflective meditations are swiftly helpful in subduing scattering and excitement, immediately return to the object of meditation. However, just as in the case of meditations designed to counteract laxity, you should not expect them to be immediately effective. Be patient with them. Give them some time. Spend some time in these reflective meditations at your leisure, or just before you go to bed at night. Become more accustomed to them and you will very likely find that the excitement and scattering will diminish the following day. The more you become familiar with reflective meditations, the more benefit they will bring to your practice.

There are physical antidotes to excitement as well. You might try wearing warmer clothes, or make your room darker by dimming the light. Increase the oil and fat content of your diet. This will help counteract excitement, but don't overdo it or you might find yourself getting very sleepy.

As a forceful method for counteracting excitement, Pa-dampa Sang-gye's advice is to visualize your mind as a small sphere of darkness at your heart, to send that out of your body through the lower orifice of your own choice, and to see it dissolve into the ground. If you repeat the process a few times, it should help.

If your object of śamatha is not breath awareness but the Buddha image or anything else, counting breaths can immediately help to counteract strong excitement and scattering. However, while focusing elsewhere is, like a good band-aid, of short-term benefit, for overcoming excitement in the long run, the reflective meditations are the most effective.

## RECOGNIZING THE CAUSES OF LAXITY AND EXCITEMENT

It can be said that failing to restrain the sense doors acts as a cause for both laxity and excitement. If, for example, you become attached to visual form, you can exhaust yourself. Then when it comes time to meditate, you are tired, and tiredness gives rise to laxity. If it doesn't cause exhaustion, becoming attached to a lovely visual form can give rise to attachment, and when you sit down to meditate, the mind will go out to the things to which you are attached. The same is true for all the other senses—sound, taste, smell, touch. Lust and sexual fantasy will also exhaust your faculties and lead to laxity.

Diet is something you have to experiment with. Too much food generally leads to laxity, but in some cases it can lead to excitement as well. Too little food generally leads to excitement, but the opposite possibility also exists. If one has a tendency to develop tension, or subtle energy disturbances, it is likely that excitement will arise. If one does not have tendencies toward tension, the danger will be laxity. Your own experience will let you know what you must do.

A Tibetan proverb says that one should fill one-third of the stomach with food, one-third with water, and one-third should be left empty for the movement of energy. That can be difficult if one is strictly following the monastic rule which prohibits eating after noon. The tendency is to gorge at lunch, to feel stuffed most of the afternoon, to be empty and hungry at night, and to be famished in the morning.

One of the antidotes to excitement is meditation on a subject that depresses the mind. Reflecting on mind-depressing subjects when excitement is not prevalent can be a cause of laxity, just as a generally gloomy attitude can.

It is also said that perseverance in association with laziness can cause either laxity or excitement. What exactly does that mean? One example would be looking at your watch and saying to yourself, "Oh. In the next minute I'm supposed to start my next session. I don't really want to but I guess I should." If you start out under those conditions, it won't be long before laxity or excitement has you in its grasp.

The failure to cultivate vigilance can cause laxity as well, so it is very important to be working on that between sessions. At the beginning of a long retreat there can be a tendency to be a little depressed between sessions. So don't bear down too hard in the first weeks. Give yourself some space. After a month or so, you can start to enhance your vigilance and have tighter discipline between sessions, to be close on guard for the arising of anger and attachment towards the various sense fields.

It is also important not to enter the retreat with too high a flame of enthusiasm, for this can lead to a state of excitement, followed by exhaustion. Then, later on, the tendency to give up or procrastinate might arise. You might begin to think, "Well, I won't do it this time. I'll just wait until the next retreat. There's bound to be one some day." It is much more effective to extend your enthusiasm to encompass the entire duration of the retreat, whether it be three months, six months, or a year.

In the West we have so many wonderful buttons to push. We push a button and a message pops out of the fax machine, or we push a button and in three minutes a fully cooked dinner pops out of the microwave oven. We are accustomed to the push-button approach, we are used to getting fast results. But there is no button to push for śamatha. If you try to find one you are wasting your time. The attainment of śamatha requires a very relaxed, patient attitude from the outset. Thinking in terms of continuity and a protracted practice will, in and of itself, act as an aid to realization. The experiences themselves will arise in accordance with your own ability, but that attitude will aid any ability you have for the fruition of your practice.

In general, it is said that the absence of serenity and the absence of a disciplined or subdued quality of mental, verbal and physical actions can act as a cause for excitement.

On the physical level, the more slowly you move your body, the greater the aid to the cultivation of stability. However, if you have been accustomed to engage in a daily routine of physical exercise and feel that cutting it off would be harmful, discontinuing the exercise itself could lead to laxity. This is something you have to check out for yourselves by means of your own experience.

In terms of mental attitude, reflecting on family and relatives or thinking about all the fun and activities you might be missing out on while you are in retreat acts as a strong cause for excitement.

Intention is that faculty of awareness which moves the mind. Whether it moves the mind to obstructions or to the application of antidotes, it is intention. Vigilance is that faculty of awareness which is on guard for the arising of obstacles, both excitement and laxity. Both of these faculties must be applied with moderation and balance. An excess of intention can cause flaming enthusiasm, whereas devoting oneself exclusively to vigilance—constantly checking, analyzing, investigating and probing—will lead to excitement. Both will deter the mind from the cultivation of meditative quiescence.

## THE FIFTH FAULT: APPLICATION

When either laxity or excitement arises and has been discerned by vigilance, if you just sit there watching the process, that failure of intention to apply an antidote is non-application. In that case, non-application is a fault, and its antidote is application.

When neither laxity nor excitement arises and out of little more than habit you unnecessarily apply antidotes, the very application is, in and of itself, a fault.

## THE ANTIDOTE TO APPLICATION

The antidote to application is equanimity,* of which there are three specific types: (1) Emotional equanimity is that intermediate emotional state which is neither pleasure nor pain. (2) Immeasurable equanimity is the evenness of mind which occurs in the absence of hostility towards the enemy and attachment for a friend. (3) In the context of śamatha, equanimity in terms of application is the non-application of antidotes. It is simply not applying antidotes when antidotes need not be applied.

Equanimity is not an antidote you will find yourself applying in the early stages of the practice. It does not come into play until the eighth mental state, when the power of both laxity and excitement have been exhausted, and there is no tendency for them to arise. Applying them then is a waste of time and energy which simply obstructs and intrudes into the practice.

The chief period of application of equanimity (the application of non-application) is in the eighth mental state. At this point, it entails the release of the antidotes to laxity and excitement, which are no longer bubbling up.

## A BRIEF SUMMARY OF THE FIVE FAULTS AND EIGHT ANTIDOTES FROM TSONG-KHA-PA'S *GREAT EXPOSITION OF THE STAGES OF THE PATH*

As one first begins the practice, the first fault is laziness. One does not apply oneself to concentration, one does not meditate. To overcome laziness, apply the four antidotes: pliancy, enthusiasm, aspiration and faith.

Once one is meditating, the fault is forgetfulness. The meditator forgets the object of meditation and does not maintain concentration. That being the case, one should apply oneself to the cultivation of mindfulness, which acts as the remedy for forgetfulness.

When the mind is concentrated, the faults that arise are laxity and excitement. When the mind is subject to these faults, it is said to be dysfunctional or unserviceable. To overcome these faults, one should apply the antidote of vigilance.

When laxity and excitement continue to arise because one is not applying the remedies, the fault is non-application. To overcome this fault, one should devote oneself to the antidote of application, which is the antidote to non-application.

When one is free of laxity and excitement the fault is application, because if one applies the antidotes when it is unnecessary it distracts from concentration. The antidote for application is equanimity (non-application).

At the outset of the practice it is difficult to gain any stability whatsoever on the object of meditation. At this initial level, one should give major emphasis to the cultivation of mindfulness.

In the second phase of the practice, as mindfulness becomes

stronger, gross scattering and excitement subside and one is likely to become vulnerable to gross laxity. At this time one must confront that fault with the application of vigilance.

In the third phase, gross laxity subsides and is replaced by the occurrence of a more subtle level of excitement and scattering. Here again, the remedy is mindfulness, and as mindfulness increases this allows a more subtle level of laxity to occur.

Once that subtler level of laxity has subsided, then there is still a problem of effort because one has become so accustomed to applying the antidotes. It is hard to break that habit. As the antidote to that effort, one must apply equanimity. It is by this means that one attains the ninth mental stage.

As one cultivates that ninth mental state with continuity, pliancy eventually arises. First it is dynamic pliancy, then it transforms into non-dynamic pliancy.

It is in this sequence and by this means that one attains meditative quiescence.

## QUESTIONS AND ANSWERS

**Q:** One person suggested the possibility of choosing subtle impermanence or emptiness as an object for śamatha. If the mind follows that route and veers off in terms of excitement, how does one recognize when subtle laxity arises, especially so since those objects have no clear boundary?

**A:** First of all, regardless of one's object of meditation, it would be very, very difficult at the outset to recognize subtle laxity. It is something that one can recognize only after one has progressed well in one's meditation.

It would be extremely difficult for emptiness and subtle impermanence to appear to the mind as objects. As an object for śamatha, the image of the Buddha is many times easier. So, on that basis alone it would be more advisable to focus on the Buddha image.

If one were to disregard that advice and choose either emptiness or impermanence as an object, one would have to precede the śamatha practice with a great deal of investigation and analysis by using reasoning to get them to appear to the mind in the first place. And how would they appear? Through the generic image* of either impermanence or emptiness; and even getting the general image, let alone the actual phenomenon itself, is very, very difficult.

Moreover, these objects can appear in the mind only after one first of all negates something else. To have that complex process as your mode of śamatha is a very difficult feat.

For example, if one were focusing on the subtle impermanence of a specific phenomenon, then first of all, one needs to recognize that there is already the appearance of permanence of that phenomenon. Then you need to refute that, and only in that way does the actual appearance of subtle impermanence occur. In both of these cases, it is not simply directing the mind to something that appears in your mind.

In the case of emptiness, one must first be concerned with the object of refutation which is true existence. Then, refuting that, the absence of true existence appears to the mind. It is rather impractical as an object of śamatha. On the other hand, if one were actually able to do it, it would be very potent.

For example, if one were able to focus very clearly on subtle impermanence, one would realize the unsatisfactory nature of all saṃsāra. This would have a very deep impact on the mind, and in that case it would be easy for renunciation, compassion and bodhicitta to arise.

Likewise, if one were able to develop śamatha focused on emptiness, insight would develop very easily. There would be great benefit in that. However, the actual implementation is extraordinarily difficult. It would be enormously difficult to get any stability upon the object at all. It's a little impractical.

**Q:** Could you elaborate a little on the technique of following the breath?

**A:** Hold the breath in the field of your awareness; follow it down through the inhalation and up through the exhalation.

During this first stage you can do the counting of twenty-one consecutive breaths, but it is optional. What is not optional, what in fact is essential, is that you allow the breath to be natural. Do not manipulate it in any way. I'll repeat that for emphasis. Count only completely natural breaths. If you force or manipulate the breath, it will bring about a surging of the winds near the heart, or other disturbances.

The object is to maintain stability on the object of meditation. Don't look at anything else. Simply note the inhalation and exhalation of the breath. Be aware of the rhythm of the breathing, but not the interrelated or associated events that are occurring in the process.

Once again, it is very important to be checking up again and again throughout the meditations. Be sure that your body, mind and breath are in a natural state. The likelihood of physical disturbance or wind disorders is much greater if you breathe with too much force or sit in an exaggerated upright and up-tight fashion. This is not just a warning for those who use breath as an object of meditation. It is equally important if you are using a Buddha image. There is a very strong tendency not to allow the breath to be natural, to force it, restrain it, or hold it because what you really want to do is pay attention to the object. An indication that you might be doing this without realizing it is finding yourself sighing deeply after a session.

**Q:** When following the breath with the eyes half opened, should the eyes be focused on anything?

**A:** No. Don't focus on anything.

**Q:** Is there a difference in the quality of the nature of one's attainment as a result of concentrating on the breath at the tip of the nose rather than following the passage of the breath in and out of the lungs, or following the up-and-down movement of the abdomen?

**A:** The great treatises, both the sūtras and the *Visuddhimagga* (a major treatise from the Theravāda Buddhist tradition), which are the major sources for the commentaries on which the contemporary tradition is based, suggest a firm and steady approach. First follow the breath up and down, and then move to the nostrils.

Whether you are focusing on the Buddha image or the breath, the placement of the object can be a potential problem. There is no certainty that focusing on the breath at the nostrils or the Buddha image at the level of the eyes will cause wind disturbances or headaches, but sometimes it happens. I have known people who had this problem and got rid of it when they moved the image down to the level of the abdomen.

Today, there are many teachers who have their students focus on the breath at the nostrils from the start. In fact, there are not many teachers who make you move the attention up and down. The reason for this is that there are not many teachers who are teaching breath awareness as a means for developing śamatha. Most are using it for the purpose of Zen or Theravāda insight meditation.

My best advice is that if you want to free your mind from the qualms of missing something important or causing yourself unnecessary problems, do just what the classic texts say to do. Start by following the breath up and down, and when you have some stability with that, shift to the nostrils.

**Q:** When we have attained some semblance of stability and are using our vigilance to guard against laxity, is it a diminishing of clarity that signals the approach of laxity? Is there any way to predict the approach before an actual loss of clarity?

**A:** Yes, it is true that the diminishing of clarity signals the approach of laxity. And, yes, you can predict its approach, but only through experience. As you continue to engage in the practice, your ability to do that will gradually grow strong.

**Q:** I am confused about the subject/object relationship. There seems to be such a close interdependence between them, I simply cannot see how it would be possible to have the subjective strength of clarity and at the same time have the object unclear.

**A:** When the mind has great zest arising from attachment or anger, awareness is very clear from its side because it is so turbulent, and yet the object can be unclear.

Say you are focusing on the Buddha image with real gusto. It is this enthusiasm that is the source of the strength of your clarity. At the same time, the Buddha you are focusing on is an unfamiliar generic image, so it is fuzzy. As you focus on it longer and longer, the image will become clearer and clearer through the force of familiarization.

Let's say you have you have a tremendous attraction to a particular person. After compulsively thinking about this person day after day, hour after hour, he or she appears extremely vividly in the mind's eye. Take a mother and an only child as an example. If the child dies, the mother's longing for her lost child could be so strong that she may even sense the child right next to her. But it only happens as a result of the mother's strong attachment, her strong sense of loss and the force of familiarization. If it is the neighbor's child that dies, neither the attachment, the loss, nor the familiarity exists.

**Q:** What size should the mental image of the Buddha be?

**A:** In general, the smaller the better. If you can do it, the best is the size of a sesame seed. If that's too difficult, the size of a grain of barley would be good. If that's too difficult, try the size of the tip of your thumb, or the size of your fist, or on the outside, about a foot tall. The smaller it is the more conducive it is for stability.

**Q:** Must the Buddha image be visualized no closer than an arm's length away? I'm nearsighted and I can see objects very clearly at a short distance.

**A:** It isn't so important to have it that far away. Bringing it closer is all right. H. H. the Dalai Lama made a comment in a public lecture in Dharamsala especially for people accustomed to wearing glasses. He said that wearing them during meditation as well will make your visualizations clearer.

**Q:** Traditionally speaking, is a student usually required to complete the ordinary and extraordinary preliminaries before engaging in intensive śamatha practice, and if so, why?

**A:** If you have done them all, that's perfect! It's wonderful. But there was no tradition in Tibet that you had to finish a hundred thousand of each of the five preliminaries before beginning śamatha.

It would be excellent to have gained a good deal of experience meditating on renunciation and bodhicitta. The critical point is for one to develop a true sense of them both. If renunciation is the motivation for one's practice of śamatha, that is a cause for the attainment of liberation. If one has developed a true sense of bodhicitta, then the practice acts as a cause for full enlightenment. Even if one has not gained some actual experience of authentic renunciation or bodhicitta prior to śamatha, if one attains śamatha, one can apply one's śamatha to the cultivation of those two and thereby can make śamatha itself a cause for liberation or full awakening. In any case, at the beginning of every session it is important to cultivate bodhicitta according to one's ability.

**Q:** You have suggested that we think of light when we go to sleep at night. If we are having a problem with excitement, should we *not* think of light when we go to bed?

**A:** The practice could increase excitement somewhat if you are very strongly inclined in that direction. At the same time, there is a great deal of benefit to be derived by visualizing light at the time of sleep. You should check it out for yourself. If you find a causal relationship between thinking of light before going to sleep and greater excitement during the day, you will know what to do.

**Q:** Could you discuss the etymology of *śamatha* and *samādhi*, and show how they are related to each other?

**A:** In this context the Sanskrit word *samādhi* translates in Tibetan as *ting nge 'dzin* and means concentration. The Sanskrit word *śamatha* translates in Tibetan as *zhi gnas*. The word *zhi* literally means "quiescence." *Gnas* (pronounced "ney") means "state" or "to abide." Because the mind has been quieted in terms of distraction and abides in a state of single-pointedness upon its object, this state is called meditative quiescence.

Now, let's talk about the relationship between samādhi and śamatha. First of all, we all have to recognize that we already have samādhi. It is concentration, and we are all able to concentrate to some extent. We don't really have śamatha, at least presumably we don't. However, as we cultivate pliancy and our concentration is empowered by it, that concentration takes on the form of meditative quiescence. So, meditative quiescence, or śamatha, is concentration that is qualified by mental and physical pliancy.

All forms of great concentration are not śamatha. There is also the samādhi of insight, or vipaśyāna. The two are related but not the same. Samādhi has the function of single-pointedly concentrating upon its object. While it is single-pointedly focused there, the function of insight is to probe the object in order to acquire greater clarity.

**Q:** In Tibetan, is there any standard dedication of merit specifically for the attainment of śamatha?

**A:**   By this merit may I swiftly
Bring to culmination the experience of śamatha;
Having done so, may I bring
Every sentient being, without exception, to that
state.

Bear in mind, however, that the experience of śamatha is not brought to culmination until you are a buddha. So, you might include in "that state" everything from śamatha all the way to full awakening.

**Q:** When following the breath, there are periods of tranquillity and happiness. This seems to happen when there is more stability and especially clarity. Are these periods the fruits of meditation, or are they a subtle form of scattering?

**A:** The happiness and tranquillity that arise in the course of meditation are indeed fruits of the meditation. They are not scattering in and of themselves. However, when they arise you should respond to them with equanimity. If you identify with them, get attached to them, get hung up on them, then they become a great disadvantage which will obstruct and disintegrate the stability that has arisen, and this will lead to other obstacles.

When you are practicing properly, joy arises naturally, spontaneously, without special effort. Do nothing at all and it will remain. When you take special notice of the joy, it retreats. When you think "Oh boy! Let's have more of that!" you might as well kiss it good-bye. It's a little like playing with a cat. When you are just walking around, the cat follows you. When you stop, turn around, and say, "Here, kitty kitty kitty," that's exactly when the cat goes away. So, do not identify with happiness. Simply continue your meditation and stability will follow you.

**Q:** If we have learned the channel exercises of the Six Yogas of Naropa, would they be good for this practice too?

**A:** If you want to do them on rare occasions just for the sake of not forgetting them, it would be all right, but do not maintain this as another practice. It will just scatter the mind.

It is helpful to avoid any superfluous activities in this practice, anything that does not directly relate to the attainment of śamatha. Even something as innocuous as collecting wood, even doing that, will obscure the mind. Also, if you are writing between sessions this will cast a veil of obscuration on the mind. If you have done it today, the mind will be somewhat obscured tomorrow.

There is a way of using the Six Yogas of Naropa as an actual technique for śamatha practice. But then you are not doing śamatha *and* that. *That* is your śamatha practice. Specifically, it is done by focusing on a certain visualization at the navel energy center. That becomes the object of meditation. In addition, you need to identify yourself with that visualized object. It is not something you look down at from above.

**Q:** Could you give some guidelines for how to set the mind immediately upon awakening, while still in bed, for making the transition into the first moments of consciousness? Would it be a good idea to immediately seek to establish your object, count breaths, take refuge, etc., as soon as possible?

**A:** The very first thing to do is to cultivate a proper motivation.

**Q:** When I notice that I am off the object and the mind does not immediately return to the object, I have a tendency to check my posture almost immediately, correcting it if necessary. Sometimes that seems to put the mind on track. If not, then I try to identify either laxity or excitement, and continue. Can you comment on this? Is checking the posture okay?

**A:** By and large, if your mind is off the object it will not be due to laxity, it will be due to distraction. So, you don't need to keep worrying whether this is laxity, or do anything further. If by force of attention alone you can bring it back, great! That is more than okay, it's good.

**Q:** My sense of hearing has become extremely sensitive. Silverware clattering and paper being crumpled seem extremely loud and harsh. Is this normal or am I weird?

**A:** This is probably fairly prevalent. It is likely that the conceptual commotion in your head is decreasing a bit, so you just have more space to hear what is coming in from the outside, and the talk is louder. It is not a result of improper practice. What is important is your response. As I mentioned before, do not identify with it or conceptually elaborate on the sound you hear.

As you go deeper into the practice and the mind becomes more drawn towards the object, then the tendency will be for the audio-perceptions to be retracted. So, rather than hearing things more vividly, you won't be hearing things that much at all.

# 10 Meditation: The Cultivation of Virtue

When an individual comes under the influence of mental distortions, the six primary* and twenty secondary mental distortions, the result is the production of all the faults and disadvantages of cyclic existence. When I say "the faults of cyclic existence," I mean all types of suffering, pain, grief and harm. In order to eradicate those problems, one needs to expel the primary and secondary mental distortions from the mind, and that is done by cultivating and increasing the wholesome power of the mind.

As long as the mind continues to be dominated by the primary or secondary mental distortions it is dysfunctional in the sense that it cannot devote itself to that which is wholesome. Meditation is the method by which one may transform the mind, allowing it to become serviceable, allowing it to be influenced by that which is wholesome. The transformation comes about as the positive qualities of bodhicitta, realization of emptiness, and renunciation are cultivated within the mind. In turn, the primary and secondary distortions are expelled. It is a way of reversing the process of habituation with mental distortion through the familiarity that comes through the nurturing of wholesome properties and faculties of the mind. It is a process that culminates in the attainment of buddhahood, of full awakening, in which all faults and disadvantages are utterly and irrevocably expelled.

In the attainment of arhatship one utterly expels the root of suffering, which is the deceived and mistaken states of mind that are specified in the six primary and twenty secondary mental distortions and collectively defined as fundamental ignorance.

Thus, the fundamental purpose of meditation is to utterly eradicate the instinctual predilection for the arising of ignorance and thereby to eradicate ignorance itself. Through further practice and more profound purification, meditation leads to the attainment of the full awakening of a buddha.

Śamatha is a cornerstone in the foundation of the process. Its purpose is to make the mind perfectly serviceable and totally efficient in terms of the cultivation of virtue.

# 11  The Stages of Cultivating the Mental States

## THE NINE MENTAL STATES

### 1. Placement

In this first mental state, the mind is bound to the object, and yet it spends most of the time off the object because it lacks the ability to remain there with any degree of continuity. This is how the practice of śamatha begins.

The text *Liberation in the Palm of Your Hands*, by Pha-bong-kha, says that in the first mental state it seems as if your thoughts have increased in quantity, that there is no stability in the mind at all, and that the mind is utterly congested. That, however, is simply how it seems. In fact, the conceptualizations have not increased in quantity, but rather, you are simply now becoming more aware of them.

Before you begin śamatha practice, you may not pay much attention to the density of your thoughts, so you simply don't notice how many there are. It may appear as if your thoughts are more congested than before, but in reality your ability to notice is simply becoming more acute. It is like moving in traffic in a downtown street. If you are not paying much attention it may not seem like there are a lot of cars. If you start looking out the window and really paying attention, you see that there are a lot of them. I have found that in ten minutes about two hundred cars pass me in downtown Seattle. That's how I spend my time in the car, counting other cars.

So, your thoughts have not increased, even though it may appear that they have. You have simply begun to recognize their existence and their volume.

## 2. *Continual Placement*

As the distractions begin to decrease there are very brief periods of continuity of placement. So, whereas in the first mental state there is hardly any continuity of awareness at all, in the second there are occasional rest periods from the onslaught of compulsive conceptualization. The mind divides its time between the object and distraction.

## 3. *Patch-like Placement*

In the previous two stages, you have been overwhelmed by the occurrence of scattering and excitement. In the third stage, you have developed the ability to recognize these problems more swiftly and to bring the mind right back to the object of meditation. It is called patch-like placement because the mind wanders off the object, you recognize its wandering and patch up the meditation process by gently returning to the object. In the third mental state the mind is usually on the object.

## 4. *Close Placement*

Prior to this point, there is a sense of separation of the meditating mind from the object of meditation. On this new level, the mind is drawn inward. The turning inward is given the name "intelligence," and it is said that now intelligence increases. The sense of separation begins to dissolve, stabilizing the inward flow of mind.

The Indian pandit Kamalaśila writes that the mind is placed upon the object by effort—that is, the mind is not being drawn totally away from the object by distractions.

According to both Ārya Asaṅga and Tsong-kha-pa, the mind is non-distracted right from the outset of the session.

Pha-bong-kha says that in the fourth mental state one has completely overcome gross excitement, so it is impossible for one to lose the object.

### 5. Subduing

At this point, the continuity of awareness of the object is maintained. You are able to recognize naturally the excellence of concentration and abide in that state. You must now subdue gross laxity, which is still very much a problem. As that process of subjugation begins, a subtle level of excitement arises. Of the three levels of excitement, the grosser has been eliminated in the previous stage. This new level to which you are now susceptible is the middle level of excitement.

### 6. Pacifying

At the previous level, you naturally see the excellence of concentration. Here in the sixth, you naturally see the faults of distraction. Excitement still occurs, that is, the middle level of excitement. Moreover, the type of distraction that occurs is not necessarily included in the mental factor of distraction, which is one of the twenty secondary mental distortions. Recognizing the faults of distraction, you pacify any inclination to ignore laxity or excitement.

### 7. Fully Pacifying

At this point, it is important to recognize and pacify the arising of attachment, unhappiness, etc. On the surface, the statement looks simple, but it needs some explanation.

Attachment in this context is straightforward. It refers to the excitement which is a form of attachment.

Unhappiness is a very specific kind of unhappiness. It is a form of regret or remorse to which one is susceptible at this stage, a looking back to your past actions with a fault-finding, critical mind. Skeletons that have been hiding in the closet are now likely to come out. You may look back at opportunities you let pass by, or thoughtless things you did that might have been done differently. Often there is a tendency to get attached to the regret, and that attachment acts as an obstacle to increasing stability. What you must remember at this moment is that the past cannot be altered, that this regret is simply another form of distraction.

One should recognize and pacify all the other types of distraction, all forms of agitation that may be motivated either by unwholesome factors like anger, jealousy and pride, or by wholesome mental factors such as compassion.

To recognize their occurrence does not mean so much their actual occurrence in the conscious mind, but rather to recognize their readiness to arise. The grosser levels may be eradicated at this point, but you also have to be sensitive to their tendency to arise. Now you will have the capacity to pacify these various obstacles even before they arise because your awareness is so clear. You will be able to avert them as they are on the verge of appearing in the consciousness.

### 8. Single-Pointed Application

Now, the mind of the individual who is striving to restrain laxity and excitement with continuity of effort naturally goes to the object without any obstruction or interference by laxity and excitement. As long as the effort is there, the mind naturally goes to its object and the obstructions do not arise.

It is said that the eighth and ninth mental states are similar in the sense that they are both free of laxity and excitement. In the eighth, however, it is necessary to expend effort to maintain mindfulness and vigilance. Through continued practice the familiarization process progresses, and then culminates in the attainment of the ninth mental state.

### 9. Meditative Equipoise

Meditative equipoise entails a level of equanimity that no longer requires the application of an antidote. The equanimity is naturally and effortlessly accomplished because you no longer have to exert yourself to cultivate mindfulness and vigilance.

You simply sit down to meditate, direct the mind to the object, and from that point on it's a free ride.

*Summary*

During the course of the movement through these mental states, from the first through the seventh, both laxity and excitement are going from gross, to subtle, to very subtle. Conversely, during that same process, the powers of mindfulness and vigilance are gradually going from weak to strong, and getting stronger.

## DIFFERENCES BETWEEN THE NINE MENTAL STATES

*First and second:* In the first mental state you cannot maintain continuity of awareness. In the second mental state you can.

*Second and third:* The distinction here is a matter of the duration of continuity. In the second mental state, there is continuity but it is still rather short in duration. In the third mental state there is a fairly good duration of continuity.

*Third and fourth:* In the third mental state it is possible to completely forget the object of meditation. In the fourth mental state you have attained the power of mindfulness. From that point forward the object will not be forgotten.

*Fourth and fifth:* In the fourth mental state the mind no longer loses the object, and it is easy to become complacent, thinking, "I've arrived! Nothing more to do. I'm not losing the object any more. Fantastic! I must have samādhi!" With this attitude, gross laxity is bound to arise.

Just to get to the fifth state, you will have to be able to handle gross laxity. Therefore, in the fifth you should not need to be especially on guard against gross laxity.

*Fifth and sixth:* It is good to try to imagine the process. By the time you have reached the fifth mental state, you have done a pretty good job of counteracting gross laxity. However, you have done such a good job that you are now rebounding off in the other direction, towards excitement. In this fifth level, you need to be especially on guard to apply antidotes for the medium level of excitement.

In the sixth mental state, you have attained the power of vigilance. Gross laxity will no longer arise. This sixth state also acts as a direct antidote for middle-level excitement and laxity.

*Sixth and seventh:* In the sixth mental state, both subtle excitement and laxity continue to manifest, but subtle excitement is a little more predominant. When you find that you are not applying the antidotes the moment you see distraction arise, you must counter this tendency. In the seventh mental state, the level of vigilance will be so acute that you will apply antidotes immediately and no longer indulge in subtle laxity and excitement.

*Seventh and eighth:* In the seventh mental state, the most subtle levels of laxity and excitement arise. As you continue to practice, however, the seventh state itself becomes the antidote for the subtlest levels of distraction.

In the eighth mental state even though the subtlest levels of laxity and excitement no longer arise, you still have to guard against them. For that very reason, effort is still required.

*Eighth and ninth:* The eighth mental state requires effort. By the sheer force of that effort, you reach a point where you no longer need to be on guard any more. At that time, it just happens effortlessly that you arrive at a state of equanimity, where even the application of effort throughout the meditation session is no longer required. Then you have arrived at the ninth mental state which requires no effort at all.

From this point forward, going into meditation and remaining there is as effortless as remaining asleep once you are asleep. Just as soon as you enter the meditation, it is still, totally free of friction.

## QUESTIONS AND ANSWERS

**Q:** If phenomena do not abide for a single moment, what does *abide* mean in the term "calm abiding"?

**A:** It means something quite different. There is no reason to confuse the terms.

In the context of impermanence the notion of abiding refers to something utterly static, something in which there is no change at all. On the other hand, when you speak of calm abiding, it is not referring to the mind or anything else being a static entity. It refers to the mind not losing its object. "Remaining" or "abiding" indicates a continuity of awareness, a continuity which is momentary. It arises moment to moment but it is an unbroken continuum without distraction.

**Q:** Is the generic image, or the appearing object, a permanent phenomenon?

**A:** There are different views on this. Apart from the Prāsaṅgika Madhyamaka school, all the Indian Buddhist philosophical schools—including the Vaibhāṣika, Sautrāntika, Vijñanavāda, and Svātantrika Madhyamaka—say that the generic image is permanent. Not permanent in the sense that it is forever, because we know that it is not; but they assert that while it is there, it does not exist as a momentary phenomenon. Why do these schools say that the generic image is permanent? Because it is the appearing image for a conceptual awareness. To illustrate the rationale of their argument, let's say you are thinking of a tree. If the generic image of the tree were impermanent, runs this argument, then the generic image would have to be a tree.

Although the Prāsaṅgika system does not assert that generic images are included in the class of non-associated, impermanent phenomena, it does maintain that they are neither form nor cognition. The basis for that statement could be related to a theory from Buddhist tantra: subtle energy arises in two fashions, both as the object and the subject. Moreover, there are different types of generic images, those of permanent phenomena and those of impermanent phenomena.

For example, a generic image of non-composite space would be a generic image of a permanent phenomenon, and that generic image itself would be permanent. Likewise, a generic image of composite space would be a generic image of an impermanent phenomenon, like a tree, and according to the Prāsaṅgika, it would therefore also be impermanent.

In tantric practice you bring forth various visualizations which are generic images. But when one approaches the culmination of this visualization process, the generic image you are creating with your mind transforms into the real thing— for example, the deity you are imagining. Previously it was a generic image, but now it transforms into the actual deity. The actual deity is impermanent in the sense of being a composite phenomenon. So, if the generic images themselves were permanent, then it would be impossible for them to transform into something impermanent.

Similarly, in the *kasiṇa** practice (e.g., of earth, water, fire, air, and space) as a method for cultivating śamatha, you focus on a generic image of earth, for example. Eventually, when you reach a fairly high attainment in this practice, the generic image that you are visualizing transforms into the actual thing. That is, the object for your meditation becomes the actual earth element and not a generic image of it.

**Q:** Could you say a few words about using mind as an object in śamatha meditation?

**A:** If you take mind as an object, it is important to focus the mind on the very clarity of the mind *without any form*. You try to remain stable there, with the resolve not to let the mind veer off elsewhere. In this particular approach to the practice, when distracting thoughts arise, the response should be to focus right on them, specifically on the very nature of the clarity of the thoughts themselves and not on their content. If you focus on the content, it will carry you away.

If you direct your mind towards the mind, all you end up with is clarity. It would be like space looking at space. If you are cultivating śamatha in that context, you direct the mind single-pointedly upon that clarity. However, first you should seek to ascertain clarity. When the clarity of the mind as an object appears to you, then, with resolve, you simply abide in that awareness. Focus on that clarity. By doing that repeatedly, it will become clearer and clearer. Generally speaking, however, it is very difficult for the mind to appear clearly to the mind.

**Q:** During sessions, maintaining stability on the Buddha image is difficult. At the same time, often the Buddha image appears quite spontaneously between sessions, not with great clarity, but nevertheless it does appear even more clearly than when I'm sitting in meditation. What is happening?

**A:** During sessions, the mind could be tight because you are trying a little too hard. Between sessions, the mind is more relaxed. When the mind eases up a bit, then the image comes. When that happens, when it arises on its own accord, go ahead and direct your mind to it. Please do not be impatient with regard to stability. It is cultivated only gradually.

**Q:** When the mind leaves the object of meditation it is called excitement. How do we recognize laxity? Is it the mind slipping off the object into a hazy state of vagueness?

**A:** When the mind loses its object altogether, this is due to the force of gross excitement or scattering. With gross laxity, the mind has not lost its object directly, it has simply lost the clarity. Again, with subtle laxity, you have not lost the object and you still have some clarity, it just does not have the strength of clarity of the meditating mind.

The function of both scattering and excitement is that the mind goes away from the object outwards. In the gross case the object is lost completely. With laxity of either type, the object is not lost, the mind withdraws and moves inward. It fades out.

## 12   Patience and Fortitude

We have already talked about laxity, excitement, and their antidotes. We have talked about the importance of devoting ourselves to having few desires, about cultivating contentment,
and about rejecting fantasies and conceptualization entailing
desire for sensual objects. These are the bricks from which
we can build the foundation of our practice. If we are to bring
that practice to its culmination, then it is also indispensable
to cultivate patience, fortitude and the forbearance of being
willing to accept the occurrence of struggle and suffering.

There are two major causes for the disturbance of the life-
sustaining subtle energy, the most crucial energy associated
with the mind. One source of an upset of this type of energy
is impatience: the lack of fortitude, forbearance and patience
in terms of accepting the suffering that comes on the path.
The second is having very great desire for, and clinging to,
the eight worldly dharmas: pleasure and pain, praise and
blame, gain and loss, fame and obscurity.

If we go back to the fundamental motivation for this practice, to attain the highest awakening for the benefit of all creatures throughout all of limitless space, if we keep this vast and
majestic motivation in mind, we can more easily cultivate a
sense of patience. We can gladly accept the unhappiness, the

pain, the struggle that occurs on the path, when we see it as an unavoidable part of attainment.

Most people accept great hardship just trying to feed themselves and their families, let alone for any grand attainment or majestic motivation. Take farmers, carpenters or fishermen as examples. Each of them must cope with physical pain, struggle, hardship, even danger. They have to put up with the violent and unpredictable forces of nature, with cold, heat, hunger, thirst, with sore and aching bodies, all of this just to get by. If they can accept the hardships of their occupations just to get by from day to day, certainly it should be within our scope to take the hardships of practice upon ourselves for the sake of benefiting all beings.

Professional athletes, boxers, football players, bicyclists and motorcyclists may endure agony just to win a game, a race, a championship, a medal. They literally risk body and life to do what they do, and they accept the hardships and the risks for something that is relatively insignificant.

In contrast, what do we have to do? We sit on a soft cushion and make sure it's nice and comfortable in back. We make sure the temperature in the room is just right—not too warm, not too cold. We have three meals a day, plus three breaks for tea. We may get a sore back or a pain in the knee now and again, we may have to deal with the noise of a truck or a distant chainsaw interrupting our meditations, we may face hardships in trying to accustom ourselves to circumstances with which we have not previously been familiar, but for the sake of striving to become a source of joy for all sentient beings and to eliminate their suffering, we should be able to put up with all of that.

Remember Śantideva's verse:

> Why be upset about something
> If it can be remedied?
> And what is the use of being upset about something
> If it cannot be remedied?

Whenever you have a problem, bring this verse to mind.

You will find that it brings about great serenity and peace.

Likewise, you should not get excited when you find yourself praised, because someone else is bound to hold you in low regard. On the other hand, when someone reviles you, someone else is bound to be thinking you are just great, so there is no reason to get excited about what anyone says. Better to remain all the while in total equanimity.

These points are extremely important. It is said that if one does not renounce the eight worldly dharmas and cultivate the patience of being willing to accept the hardships on the path, there is no possibility of attaining the culmination of the practice.

# 13 The Mental Powers and Forms of Attention

## ACCOMPLISHING THE SIX MENTAL POWERS

The Six Powers are designated at different stages along the path, but all six are generally relevant throughout the path.

### 1. The Power of Hearing

The first power is based upon hearing the teachings on śamatha, and it is with this power that one attains the first mental state.

How does that power arise? It arises through the process of understanding the teachings. Thus, the power of hearing is based on understanding the nature, function and benefits of concentration, as well as the manner of meditating upon the object. It develops and grows stronger through an understanding of the defining characteristics, the functions and the sequence of the obstacles that arise in the course of meditation, as well as the defining characteristics, functions and the sequence of antidotes for these faults.

Listening to the teachings is not sufficient. The power of hearing is mastered not just when the teachings are heard, but when they are both heard and understood.

## 2. *The Power of Reflection*

It is through the power of reflection that the second mental state is attained.

You develop the power of reflection by accustoming yourself to the practice, engaging in it repeatedly, and returning to the object again and again by implementing the teachings that you have heard. Actually, you have begun to cultivate this power even before engaging in meditation, but it is in the practice that the true power of reflection becomes evident.

## 3. *The Power of Mindfulness*

The chief function of the power of mindfulness is to prevent the mind from wavering off the object, and it is through this power that the third and fourth mental states are attained.

Unquestionably, the power of mindfulness is needed in the first two states as well, but it is in the third and fourth that it clearly manifests, when the major obstacles, scattering and excitement, are causing you to forget the object. Clearly manifesting at this point, the power of mindfulness counteracts excitement and scattering and brings the mind back to the object.

## 4. *The Power of Vigilance*

It is said that the fifth and sixth mental states are attained through the power of vigilance.

The chief opponent power for the occurrence of laxity is vigilance. When the mind has become stabilized on the object through the force of mindfulness you will not lose it. And yet, while you are focused on the object, the mind has a tendency to become lax, and to counter this you need vigilance.

In the fifth state, gross laxity is the greatest problem and vigilance is laxity's most effective antidote. In the sixth state, gross laxity has begun to subside and the middle-level excitement and laxity are likely to arise, with excitement being the greater of the two. It is only by refining and sharpening the power of vigilance that either of these two faults can be defeated.

## 5. *The Power of Effort*

It is said that the seventh and eighth mental states are attained by the power of effort.

By the time you have reached the sixth mental state, you are endowed with the power of vigilance. However, while this power has come into its fullness, it is still possible for a subtle level of excitement and laxity to arise. This can even occur in the seventh mental state. Therefore, having the power of vigilance does not mean that you don't need to implement it any more. On the contrary, it means that you must apply the powers of vigilance and mindfulness you have already perfected, and those powers are implemented through the power of effort.

In the seventh mental state, with a developed and sensitive power of vigilance, you are able to ascertain when either laxity or excitement are on the verge of arising. With the exertion of effort, you are able to apply the antidote instantly, snuffing out the faults before they ever have the chance to manifest. It is through this process that you go on to attain the eighth mental state.

## 6. *The Power of Familiarization*

By the continual application of effort throughout the eighth mental state, the process of meditation is carried out with less and less expense of energy. Rather than applying a particular antidote, you simply carry on with a diminishing degree of effort, fulfilling the necessity of familiarizing yourself with the practice. Eventually when the meditation becomes totally effortless, you have attained the ninth mental state.

### *An Exercise*

To test your grasp of the six mental powers and nine mental states, work through them from the last to the first. Start with the ninth mental state, where there is equanimity. Recall that this equanimity is attained by the power of familiarization. And how did you get there? This was done by the power of effort. Effort of what type? The effort of the continual application of mindfulness and vigilance applied during the seventh and eighth mental states. And what is the difference between the seventh and eighth mental states? In the seventh there is the possibility that either excitement or laxity could arise, so as they are on the verge of arising you need to be aware with effort to apply mindfulness and vigilance. Then carry on in reverse order, all the way down to the first mental state.

## THE FOUR FORMS OF ATTENTION

### 1. Forceful Attention

This form of attention is the requirement of gross effort at the outset of the practice and the individual sessions. It is a forceful placement, holding, apprehension or maintaining of the object. It is present during the first and second mental states.

### 2. Interrupted Attention

The form of attention that occurs during the middle five mental states is called interrupted attention. From the third to the seventh mental state, the mind is by and large on the object. In contrast to the forceful attention of the first and second mental states, here the attention is only interrupted intermittently by excitement and laxity. Thus, interrupted attention is a less intense form of forceful attention.

### 3. Uninterrupted Attention

In the eighth mental state, because the mind is no longer interrupted at all by either laxity or excitement, the form of attention in that state is called uninterrupted attention. It functions only in the eighth mental state.

### 4. Spontaneous Attention

In the ninth mental state no effort whatsoever is required and for that reason the form of attention that occurs here is called spontaneous.

**PART IV**

**THE CRITERIA FOR
HAVING ATTAINED
ŚAMATHA**

# 14  Pliancy

## THE FIRST AND LAST ANTIDOTE

Pliancy is a quality you already have, something that is present as we start the practice, from the very first mental state. It is the first antidote to laziness; however, in the early stages of the practice it exists in such a subtle form that it does not manifest in a recognizable way.

In the ninth mental state, by the process of familiarization over a long period of time, pliancy is fully manifested in a very recognizable way. In this well-developed state, it acts as an antidote to the mental and physical dysfunction that is an obstacle to the practice of meditation.

As we progress through the nine mental states, this dysfunction gradually decreases. Upon the attainment of the ninth mental state it reaches the point at which it is on the verge of disappearing. As those forms of dysfunction have been decreasing in power, pliancy has been increasing in power, and just as the dysfunction is about to disappear, pliancy is about to fully manifest itself.

## SIGNS OF PLIANCY

Generally speaking, mental pliancy arises first and is followed by physical pliancy. The first sign of mental pliancy is a spontaneous mental joy. It arises, it increases, and as it continues to grow, the presence of a new form of subtle energy indicates the arising of physical pliancy. One of the first signs of physical pliancy is a sensation comparable to the slight pressure you would feel if someone were to place a warm hand on your freshly shaved head. This subtle energy is unprecedented. As it courses through the body, it creates a sensation of fullness throughout the body.

As the initial joy of physical pliancy increases, it activates a new level of mental bliss. The mental bliss compounds the physical, they influence each other with increasing intensity. As you can see, this is getting rather potent. The pliancy is very dynamic, and gets stronger and stronger, building toward a peak.

Eventually, this dynamic pliancy tapers off, and one attains a subtle pliancy that is called "special pliancy."

At what moment is śamatha actually attained? It is attained after the mounting of pliancy has settled. First it swells increasingly as it moves about. Then there is a moment of tapering off, and when that occurs, śamatha has been attained.

In this context, we can draw on another etymology of the Tibetan translation of *śamatha*, *zhi gnas*. There is an "abiding" (*gnas*) following the "pacification" (*zhi*) of the movement of pliancy.

The statement that śamatha is attained following the attainment of pliancy is firmly based on the Buddha's own teachings in the *Saṃdhinirmocanasūtra*. In this sūtra, Maitreya asks Buddha Śākyamuni what he would call the achievement of focused awareness prior to the attainment of mental and physical pliancy. The Buddha replies that this is not called śamatha, but is merely a mental factor similar to śamatha. It is not the real thing, because, as we can see from the formulation of the question, mental and physical pliancy have not yet been attained.

The need of the ninth mental state as the cause for pliancy is pointed out by Maitreya in his text *The Examination of the Center and the Extremes:*

> On the ninth mental state, following the attainment of both physical and mental pliancy, there is a form of attention which is called śamatha.

Recognizing that there are two levels of mental and physical pliancy, first the moving form and then the special form, we can pinpoint two elements that make up the criteria of having attained śamatha. First, one must have attained the ninth mental state, as a state of concentration in which the application of either mindfulness or vigilance requires no effort. Second, one must have attained the special form of mental and physical pliancy.

## QUESTIONS AND ANSWERS

**Q:** If one is free of laxity and excitement in both the eighth and the ninth mental states, why do we need continually to maintain mindfulness and vigilance in the eighth?

**A:** In the eighth mental state there is still a predisposition for their arising. They can be on the verge of arising. You may have gotten rid of the manifestations of laxity and excitement, but you have not cut them at the root. They are still potentially there.

**Q:** At the sixth mental state, when we succumb to subtle laxity and excitement, is that because it is so subtle that we aren't able to recognize it immediately, or is it because we fail to apply the appropriate antidote?

**A:** Both can still arise, and at that stage subtle excitement is easier to recognize than subtle laxity. The greatest danger is that you are so involved in concentration that you may simply not care about the arising of subtle laxity. It doesn't appear to be harmful at all. Your concentration is stable, it appears to be great, so you can say, "So what. Who cares?"

When you fail to apply the antidote, what happens is that you think you are practicing concentration, but in fact you are practicing concentration mixed with subtle laxity. You can continue in that state for a long time and feel perfectly wonderful, but it will totally disintegrate your practice. It is said that you can stay in this state for seven days and seven nights in a single session. Your senses are shut down, you don't see anything, you don't hear anything, so it is easy to congratulate yourself and think: "I have arrived!"

You may have arrived, but unfortunately you went somewhere you didn't want to go. Subtle laxity is still there, and it will continue to be there unless you are on guard for it. It arises in both the sixth and seventh mental states. Even in the seventh, if you do not apply the antidotes it can still arise. The danger is still there.

**Q:** Please correct me if I am wrong. I understood you to say that there was no real attainment possible without first attaining śamatha. Yet, there seem to be many other attainments without śamatha. Is this a matter of semantics or am I missing something?

**A:** The Abhidharma literature says that there are three levels of understanding, one arising from hearing, one from reflection, and one from meditation. In the context of Sūtrayāna practice, the understanding arising from meditation does not occur until one has attained śamatha. In terms of the Mahāyāna Five Paths, without śamatha it is not possible to attain anything from the medium stage of the Mahāyāna Path of Accumulation on up.

In the context of the Hīnayāna path, without śamatha it is not possible to ascend to the Path of Preparation or beyond.

In tantric practice, the attainment of śamatha immediately follows the culmination of the stage of generation. Therefore, it is clearly possible to reach the culmination of the stage of generation without śamatha. It is not possible, however, to attain the realization of the stage of completion without śamatha.

There are many realizations, in terms of both sūtra and tantra, that can be attained without śamatha—renunciation, bodhicitta, realization of emptiness are examples. Even when you are in the ninth mental state, you still have not attained śamatha, but just to get there you *have* attained the first eight.

To suggest that no realizations can be attained without śamatha would be to disparage the realizations or attainments of all those who have not attained śamatha. That would be disparaging almost everyone in the world, which I would like to avoid. The important thing to remember is that the attainment of śamatha will make any further attainments more stable, more profound.

**Q:** Is the goal of śamatha practice a non-dual state of awareness in which the observer ceases to be, in the sense of being a subjective witness? That is to say, is the observer absorbed in the observed? Is there only one, or does the sense of observer and object remain to the end?

**A:** Upon the attainment of śamatha, the object appears neither separate from nor identical with the subject. It is just like looking at something with eyes. You don't have any conceptual program indicating that it's different, or any kind of identification concluding that it is the same. It is just there.

# 15  A Few Final Words

As I have said before, hardships will undoubtedly arise in your practice. That is why it is so very important to cultivate the patience to accept whatever arises in the course of the path.

Strangely enough, one of the greatest obstacles can be success. Because we are so deeply enmeshed in the eight worldly dharmas, we tend to be immediately aroused any time any type of realization or deeper experience arises. Suddenly our minds are flooded with self-serving thoughts: "Oh, I am someone very special. I will most certainly become a celebrity!" That rush of self-importance, that pride of accomplishment, that exalted sense of self, is so easy to acquire and so very difficult to shake off or subdue.

For example, it is not at all unusual to hear practitioners refer to śamatha as if it were something that can be easily attained. Often, when meditators attain just a little taste of stability, they say, "I've got śamatha!" when in actuality what they are doing is mistaking stability for śamatha. As their stability increases and they experience the arising of even a small degree of physical and mental bliss, the suggestion that they still have work to do in order to attain śamatha goes right over their heads. Responding to progress with pride or conceit puts us in a state of mind where we are not ready to listen and not able to hear.

Another major obstacle we must beware of is the appearance of visions. Many of us get confused and mixed up when we are visited by visions that normally appear to the mind in the course of meditation. Once they have appeared, it is very easy for ordinary people like us, people who are not very advanced along the path, to respond with pride. Pride can lead us to identify those visions as great signs of progress, and that in turn can make us very unreceptive when even our trusted teachers tell us we have not attained what we think we have attained. If we allow ourselves to fall into this trap, our progress becomes our downfall, because rather than continuing to ascend, our practice will inevitably deteriorate.

It is a paradox, isn't it? What appears to us to be progress can become an obstacle or a form of interference. This is not the case just with those of us who are beginning on the path, it happens to those who have had profound realizations. It has happened that bodhisattvas who are striving with great courage along the path to enlightenment will apparently have a vision of the Buddha that is actually Māra* appearing in the form of the Buddha. That very vivid being that appears to be the Buddha will turn to the bodhisattva and say, "You are on the wrong path. If you follow it you are really going to destroy yourself. You must get off this quickly or you will lose your way altogether." The bodhisattva will hear these words and see them coming from the mouth of the Buddha. Yogis of great experience and wisdom must use all their resources to retain their equilibrium in the face of these kinds of obstacles, and practitioners who have very great faith but not much learning are especially susceptible to them.

There are an infinite number of wrong paths we might mistakenly follow in this practice, and they wear subtle disguises. If we wanted to go from here to Seattle, there are all kinds of roads, all sorts of paths we could follow that would *not* take us there. We can see those roads. In this visible world there are signposts that show us the right way and the right road to take. There are other travelers along the way who can guide us if we get lost.

In the journey of śamatha there are no visible paths, there are no signposts to follow. There are, however, other travelers who can guide us. They are the teachers who have passed the directions on to us: Tsong-kha-pa, Maitreya, Asaṅga, and all the others on whose experience and writings these teachings of the past eight days have been based. That is why it is so important that we gather the information, organize it, learn it. That is why it is absolutely essential that we cultivate the power of hearing to engrave these teachings in our minds.

The great yogi Milarepa faced incredible hardships and was molested by demons of great strength. He stood firm in the face of all difficulties, overcame the obstacles, and gained great realizations not in spite of them but through them. To subdue those obstacles as he did, each of us must have great equanimity in the face of whatever occurs, we must not become attached to or repelled by what may appear to be good or bad, and we must focus single-pointedly on the meditation. To accomplish that task requires a complete, profound understanding of the teachings and a strong sense of purpose. I urge you to cultivate all these qualities and cultivate the practice with continuity.

# Dedication

We have arrived at this place and in this time and enter into this practice with a good deal of inspiration, determination, and courage. I feel fortunate to be here, as I know you do, and it is important that we respond to this good fortune with rejoicing. If we can engage in this practice of śamatha with a motivation of cultivated bodhicitta, let alone actual spontaneous bodhicitta, then—whether we fall ill, or even die, or whatever happens over the duration of our practice—it will be something of meaning and benefit.

Now, I ask you to join me in dedicating the merits of the giving as well as receiving the teachings to our attainment of full awakening in order to dispel the suffering of innumerable sentient beings who are in a state of grief and unhappiness. With that as our fundamental dedication, let us also dedicate the merits of this event for our reaching the culmination of śamatha practice and for being free of obstacles, that this world may be covered with great meditators, that there may be prosperity and happiness for all sentient beings, and that the Dharma may flourish.

Moreover, in that it is extremely profound, meaningful and pure to dedicate one's merit towards exactly the things to which the Buddhas of the three times have dedicated their merit,

let us do that now; and let us pray that all of this will be accomplished by the truth of the Triple Gem, the truth of ultimate reality, and the power of altruism.

# Glossary

**Abhidharma:** One of the three "baskets" of the Buddhist teachings; includes a variety of topics ranging from psychology to physiology and metaphysics.

**Access concentration:** (Tib. *nyer bsdogs*) Also known as threshold concentration; a state of concentration that immediately precedes and provides access to actual meditative stabilization.

**Application:** (Tib. *'dud byed*) The exertion of effort to overcome the five faults; the fifth fault as well as the antidote to non-application.

**Aspiration:** (Tib. *'dun pa*) A wholesome wish for attainment and realization; one of the antidotes to laziness.

**Bodhicitta:** (pronounced "bo-di-chit-ta") The altruistic aspiration to achieve spiritual awakening for the benefit of all sentient beings.

**Bodhisattva:** A person who is continually, naturally and effortlessly motivated by bodhicitta.

**Clarity:** (Tib. *gsal cha*) The vividness of the awareness as well as the object in meditative practice.

**Concentration:** (Tib. *ting nge 'dzin*) Continuous, single-pointed focusing on a designated object.

**Dākas and dākinīs:** Male and female enlightened beings who sometimes appear in visionary experience and sometimes manifest in human form.

**Devas:** Gods dwelling in the sensual realm, the realm of form, or the formless realm.

**Dhyāna:** Any of four levels of meditative stabilization in the form realm.

**Dysfunction:** (Tib. *gnas ngan len*) A feeling of heaviness and lethargy in body and mind; a state in which it is hard to arouse the mind to wholesome activity.

**Eight worldly dharmas:** The concern to encounter pleasure, material gain, praise and fine reputation, and to avoid pain, material loss, blame and poor reputation.

**Enthusiasm:** (Tib. *brtson 'grus*) A mental factor; a state of happiness which delights in virtue; one of the four antidotes to laziness.

**Equanimity:** (Tib. *btang snyoms*) A state of calm and composure in which one no longer applies antidotes to faults that no longer arise.

**Excitement:** (Tib. *rgod pa*) A state of mind that occurs when focusing upon a desirable object with which one is previously acquainted, causing the mind to be scattered outwards; one of the five faults.

**Faith:** (Tib. *dad pa*) A conviction and confidence in those truths that are not evident or obvious and whose realization may lie beyond the experience of the believer; one of the four antidotes to laziness.

**Fifty-one mental factors:** A list of a wide array of mental factors, wholesome, unwholesome and karmically neutral.

**Forgetfulness:** (Tib. *brjed ngas*) The losing of the object under the influence of mental distortions; one of the five faults.

**Four remedial powers:** (1) The power of remorse for an unwholesome deed; (2) the power of the resolve to avoid such deeds from now on; (3) the power of "reliance," entailing taking refuge in the Three Jewels and cultivating compassion; (4) the power of applying purificatory antidotes, e.g., the Vajrasattva meditation.

**Generic image:** (Tib. *don spyi*) A mental image that arises in conceptual cognition.

**Gross excitement:** (Tib. *rgod pa rags pa*) A level of excitement in which the mind remains attached to its object of craving despite the fact that one has applied antidotes to excitement.

**Gross laxity:** (Tib. *bying ba rags pa*) A form of laxity which entails the lack of lucidity and strength of clarity; when the mind is under its influence forceful apprehension of the object has been lost or has largely slacked off.

**Guru:** Spiritual mentor.

**Highest yoga tantra:** The most subtle and profound of the four classes of Buddhist tantra.

**Hinayāna:** Literally the "lesser vehicle" of Buddhism, so called due to the limited motivation of striving for liberation from the cycle of existence for oneself alone.

**Intelligence:** (Tib. *shes rab*) The process through which the mind is turned inward.

**Intention:** (Tib. *'du byed pa*) A mental factor having the function of directing the mind inward and the mental factors with which it is conjoined towards a given object.

**Karma:** Action, or more specifically, the volition behind an intentional action.

**Kasina:** Literally the term means "entirety"; in this text it refers chiefly to the external representation of, for example, one of the five elements as one's object of meditation.

**Lama:** The Tibetan translation of the Sanskrit *guru*.

**Laxity:** (Tib. *bying ba*) A mental factor which is distracted inwardly, while cultivating virtue, due to a diminishing of the strength of clarity.

**Laziness:** (Tib. *le lo*) A mental factor identified as lack of delight in the wholesome or virtuous; laziness is attached to sloth and does not delight in virtue.

**Lethargy:** (Tib. *rmugs pa*) A mental factor included within ignorance; one of the six primary mental obstructions.

**Mahāsiddhas:** People who are greatly accomplished in terms of the various siddhis, or extraordinary abilities, especially the "supreme siddhi" of enlightenment.

**Mahāyāna:** Literally the "greater vehicle" within Buddhism, so called due to expansive motivation of striving for full spiritual awakening for the benefit of all sentient beings.

**Mahāyāna Five Paths:** Five sequential paths of spiritual practice, beginning with the initial experience of spontaneous, unforced bodhicitta, and culminating in the experience of full awakening. The paths are called the paths of accumulation, preparation, seeing, meditation, and no more training.

**Mantra:** Syllables recited for their spiritually transformative power.

**Māra:** The embodiment of evil in Buddhist theory and narratives, often manifesting to detract people from the spiritual path.

**Mental states:** (Tib. *sems gnas*) Nine stages of progress in the development of śamatha, discussed in terms of the attenuation of excitement and laxity and the enhancement of attentional stability and clarity.

**Mindfulness:** (Tib. *dran pa*) The ability to maintain continuity of awareness of the object.

**Nirmāṇakāya:** The "emanation body" of a Buddha; the forms a Buddha takes when appearing to ordinary beings.

**Nirvāṇa:** Liberation from cyclic existence.

**Non-application:** (Tib. *'du mi byed pa*) The failure to apply the antidotes when laxity and excitement arise.

**Non-discursive stability:** (Tib. *mi rtog pa'i gnas cha*) Attentional stability that is free from ideation.

**Obstructions to omniscience:** (Tib. *shes bya'i sgrib pa*) Very subtle obstructions, including predispositions to mental afflictions that obstruct the attainment of buddhahood.

**Pliancy:** (Tib. *shin tu sbyangs pa*) (1) Physical pliancy is a sensation one feels in the body; a very pleasurable tactile sensation associated with the movement of subtle energies or prana within the body. (2) Mental pliancy is an actual mental event which renders the body and mind "fit for action" and serviceable.

**Prana:** Subtle, phenomenological energies experienced in the body, which are closely related to states of awareness.

**Pranic disturbances:** Disturbances of prana, such that these energies do not flow properly in their respective channels.

**Pūja:** Devotional spiritual practice, oriented around making offerings to the enlightened beings.

**Samādhi:** (Tib. *ting nge 'dzin*) Meditative concentration which provides the basis for cultivating insight.

**Śamatha:** (Tib. *zhi gnas;* pronounced "sha-ma-ta") Meditative quiescence or calm abiding; a form of meditation which creates a stable mind capable of focusing single-pointedly on emptiness or any other phenomenon; access to the first meditative stabilization.

**Saṃsāra:** Cyclic existence, characterized in the case of humans by the cycle of birth, aging, sickness, and death.

**Scattering:** (Tib. *phro ba*) Mental turbulence not originating from attachment.

**Serviceability:** (Tib. *las su rung ba*) A buoyancy of the body and mind; a state in which the mind is easily aroused to engage in wholesome activity.

**Siddhi:** Extraordinary powers, such as walking on water and flying through the air, that can be developed through meditation and other means.

**Six primary mental distortions:** Attachment, anger, pride, doubt, ignorance and mistaken views.

**Six-Session Guru Yoga:** A tantric devotional and meditative practice in the Gelug tradition designed to help one keep the tantric vows and pledges.

**Sleepiness:** (Tib. *gnyid*) The mental factor tending toward sleep.

**Stability:** (Tib. *gnas cha*) Continuity of mindfulness on one's chosen object.

**Strength of clarity:** (Tib. *gsal cha'i ngar*) The strength of the clarity with which the mind apprehends the object.

**Subtle excitement:** (Tib. *rgod pa phra mo*) A form of excitement in which the mind is not scattered away from the object although the awareness does not remain entirely on the object.

**Subtle laxity:** (Tib. *bying ba phra mo*) A form of laxity in which there is some lucidity and strength of clarity, but in which the force of apprehension of the object has only slightly slacked off.

**Sūtra:** An exoteric discourse attributed to the Buddha.

**Sūtrayāna:** The "sūtra vehicle," of exoteric Buddhist theory and practice, in contrast to the esoteric Vajrayāna.

**Tantra:** A class of esoteric teachings and practices in Mahāyāna Buddhism, distinguished from the more exoteric class of the sūtras.

**Vajrayāna:** The esoteric vehicle within Mahāyāna Buddhism, emphasizing the transmutation, rather than the simple suppression and elimination, of mental afflictions.

**Vigilance:** (Tib. *shes bzhin*) The mental faculty of guarding or watching over the meditative process to recognize if either excitement or laxity has occurred.

# Further Reading

Buddhaghosa. *Visuddhimagga*. Translated as *The Path of Purification* by Ñāṇamoli Thera. 4th ed. Kandy: Buddhist Publication Society, 1979.

Goldstein, Joseph, and Jack Kornfield. *Seeking the Heart of Wisdom: The Path of Insight Meditation*. Boston: Shambhala, 1987.

Gunaratana, Henepola. *The Path of Serenity and Insight*. Columbia, Missouri: South Asia Books, 1985.

Lati Rinbochay, Denma Locho Rinpoche, Leah Zahler and Jeffrey Hopkins. *Meditative States in Tibetan Buddhism*. London: Wisdom Publications, 1983.

Lodrö, Geshe Gedün. *Walking through Walls: A Presentation of Tibetan Meditation*. Translated and edited by Jeffrey Hopkins, co-edited by Anne C. Klein and Leah Zahler. Ithaca, New York: Snow Lion Publications, 1992.

Ñāṇamoli Thera. *Mindfulness of Breathing*. 3rd ed. Kandy: Buddhist Publication Society, 1973.

Takpo Tashi Namgyal. *Mahāmudrā: The Quintessence of Mind and Meditation*. Translated by Lobsang P. Lhalungpa. Boston and London: Shambhala, 1986.

Vajirañāṇa Mahāthera. *Buddhist Meditation in Theory and Practice*. 2nd ed. Kuala Lumpur: Buddhist Missionary Society, 1975.